CONTENTS

McGraw-Hill School Division

UNIT 2: NATURE LINKS

McGraw-Hill School Division

UNIT 1: TELL ME MORE

McGraw-Hill School Division

UNIT 2: THINK IT THROUGH

UNIT 3: TURNING POINTS

McGraw-Hill School Division

Story Elements

Think about one of your favorite stories. What character do you remember the most? (*Characters*** are the people in a story.) Where did the story take place? (The *setting* is where and when the story takes place.)**

Write a paragraph about your favorite character. How did the character look? What important action did he or she perform in the story? What makes your character special? What did your character do to make it a good story? Where and when did the story take place? Did the time or place matter? Why or why not?

_____

_____

_____

_____

_____

Act out your character to see if your classmates can guess who the character is and where the story happens. (To do this activity, remember to act out a well-known story and character.) Take a cat stuck in a tree for example. How would you act out the ways it gets into mischief? (Obviously, it is because the cat is curious, but how would you show its actions?) What if your character is feeling fear or anger? How would you show these feelings?

_____

_____

_____

_____

McGraw-Hill School Division

At Home: Take a favorite story or stories and discuss the illustrations that best show the characters acting in important settings.

Vocabulary

astonished	enormous	journey
scattered	surrounded	towering

Imagine you're far from home in a place of your choice. Write a letter home using some of the words in the box. Remember to include details about the places you are seeing.

Story Comprehension

Grandfather's Journey

Work with a partner. Choose a setting from "Grandfather's Journey." Draw one detail about the setting. Then choose a title for your illustration.

At Home: Draw a timeline together tracing some of the main events in Grandfather's life.

2–3

Book 3.1/Unit 1
Grandfather's Journey

Use Book Parts

Suppose you wanted to write a book about holidays in the United States. There are several ways you could organize your book into chapters. One way would be to have a chapter for each holiday. Think of other ways your book could be organized, and write them below.

_____

_____

Now use your method of organization to make a sample table of contents for your book. Use another sheet of paper if you need more room.

Holidays in the United States
Table of Contents

_____

_____

_____

_____

_____

_____

_____

_____

_____

_____

_____

McGraw-Hill School Division

At Home: Read through the table of contents of a book. Then quiz each other on the information that can be found in the book, and how that information is organized.

Story Elements

The author wrote about his grandfather as if he had interviewed him for a long time. He had many details to put into his story.

Interview three people who you know and who have traveled. Ask each person to name a place and tell you something each remembers about the trip. Take notes on each person in the space provided below.

_____   _____   _____

_____   _____   _____

_____   _____   _____

_____   _____   _____

_____   _____   _____

Write about one of these places that you would also like to visit and tell why.

_____

_____

_____

_____

_____

_____

At Home: Discuss the difference in reading books in a series and watching a weekly TV show. Ask: How do you get to know the characters? Are they always the same? How do the authors and producers make them different in each book or show?

McGraw-Hill School Division

Make Predictions

Some things that happen can change everyone's life. In "Grandfather's Journey," the war started. "Bombs fell from the sky and scattered our lives like leaves in a storm." Write what you think might have happened to the author and his grandfather if the war had not started.

_____

_____

_____

_____

Would you guess that the author of the story would feel the same way about journeys that his grandfather did? Why or why not?

_____

_____

_____

_____

Book 3.1/Unit 1
Grandfather's Journey

At Home: Have students make predictions about what they might do next Saturday.

6

Compound Words

Compound words are made by putting two words together. The words *basket* and *ball* make the word basketball.

Use the words below to write as many new compound words as you can.

grand	steam	sick	river	sea	father	ship
boat	coast	land	end	parent	home	week

_____   _____

_____   _____

_____   _____

_____   _____

Choose some of these compound words and write a story about someone you know who has gone on a journey.

_____

_____

_____

_____

_____

Create a class compound word chart. Display it in the classroom. Add words to the chart during the year.

At Home: Ask students to think of compound words that will have something to do with what they will do that day.

Book 3.1/Unit 1
Grandfather's Journey

7

McGraw-Hill School Division

Problem and Solution

For most problems there are solutions. Some solutions are simple and predictable. Other solutions can be part of a plot, or plan, of a story. Read each of the problems below and choose the solution that you think would make the best story. Explain why. Then choose one problem and solution and write a paragraph about it.

Problem

1. A new student just moved into the school. The new student is sitting on the playground alone.

Solution

1. **(A)** A high flying ball comes sailing at her and she catches it. The others swarm around her.

1. **(B)** A girl asks the child to play.

_____

_____

2. A friend is coming over to play, but your room is a terrible mess.

2. **(A)** First, you have to find the missing baseball card your friend expects you to return.

2. **(B)** You quickly clean your room so you can play.

_____

_____

3. You will have a spelling bee tomorrow, but you have not studied for it yet.

3. **(A)** You start studying and ask your sister for help.

3. **(B)** You take your spelling list to a spelling owl who lives in a tree down the street.

_____

_____

Book 3.1/Unit 1
Phoebe and the Spelling Bee

At Home: Discuss ways of solving problems. Suggest that, in stories, solutions are not always practical. Talk about some stories that solve a problem creatively.

8

Vocabulary

The correct spelling of some words is difficult to remember. Make up a short and funny story using these words and illustrate it.

continue	correct	legend	unusual	embarrass	groaning

Do you find these words difficult to spell? Tell how you can remember them.

Story Comprehension

Phoebe had a special way of studying her spelling words. Turn Phoebe's solution into a play. Have each person in your group take a character. First, find lines from the story for your character. Then predict what your character might say, and write some lines on your own. Act out the play you have written. Give the play a new ending.

At Home: Ask students to cut challenging spelling words out of magazines. Discuss how you can remember these words.

McGraw-Hill School Division

Use a Glossary

A glossary is a small dictionary in the back of a book.

As in a dictionary, words are defined in the glossary. An example sentence is usually given for each word. Some glossaries show the page where the word can be found. Use the sample glossary below to answer each of the questions.

Earth The only planet known in our solar system to have all the conditions and materials needed for human life. There are many forms of plant and animal life on *Earth.* (Page 18)

endangered A living thing that may become extinct. The manatee is an *endangered* animal. (Page 43)

erosion The washing away of the land. The roots of trees can help stop *erosion.* (Page 25)

evaporate To change from a liquid to a gas. Water *evaporates* to form water vapor. (Page 22)

extinct When all animals of one kind die. There are no dinosaurs, such as brontosauruses, today, because these animals are *extinct.* (Page 44)

F

flat teeth Teeth that are good for grinding food. Many plant-eating dinosaurs had *flat teeth.* (Page 42)

fossil Remains or imprint of a once-living thing. Brontosaurus footprints in rock are one kind of *fossil.* (Page 45)

1. Look up the word *endangered* and write another example sentence

   for it. _____

   _____

2. Look up the word *fossil* and write another example sentence for it.

   _____

   _____

3. If you decided to add the word *everglade* to this glossary, between

   what two words would it be placed? _____

4. Where do you think you might find out more about a brontosaurus?

   _____

   _____

At Home: Start a journal of third grade words. Have students put in words worth remembering from anything they study in class. Write definitions and, later, put the words in A-B-C order.

McGraw-Hill School Division

Problem and Solution

Most problems have solutions. Some solutions are good. Other solutions are not so good. For each problem Phoebe had, write her solution. Then tell whether the solution was good or not so good.

1. Katie tried to help Phoebe spell brontosaurus.

_____

_____

2. Katie called Phoebe to find out how she was doing with her spelling list.

_____

_____

3. Ms. Ravioli announced a mock spelling bee. Phoebe was nervous.

_____

_____

4. Phoebe felt very bad about lying to Katie.

_____

_____

_____

5. Ms. Ravioli started the spelling bee.

_____

_____

_____

At Home: Debate Phoebe's and Katie's ways of learning spelling. Which works better?

Book 3.1/Unit 1
Phoebe and the Spelling Bee

12

Make Predictions

A prediction is a good guess about what will happen in the future. You need some good information to make good predictions. Think about what Phoebe did in "Phoebe and the Spelling Bee." Then make a prediction for each question below.

1. Do you predict that Katie will do well in future spelling bees?

_____

_____

_____

2. Do you predict that Phoebe will continue to put off studying her

spelling? _____

_____

_____

3. Do you predict that Phoebe and Katie will continue to be friends?

_____

_____

_____

4. Do you predict that some of the class will use Phoebe's method for

learning spelling words? _____

_____

_____

_____

McGraw-Hill School Division

Book 3.1/Unit 1
Phoebe and the Spelling Bee

At Home: Make up two prediction questions about
another story or TV show.

13

Prefixes

Word parts, such as *un* and *re* are called prefixes. The prefixes *un* and *re* can change the meaning of words. For example, *un* means "not" as in unable, or "opposite" as in uncover. The word part *re* means "again," as in refill, or "back" as in replay.

Use *un* or *re* to change the meaning of the words below. Then write sentences using the words you created.

1. _____ lucky

_____

2. _____ usual

_____

3. _____ happy

_____

4. _____ check

_____

5. _____ fill

_____

6. _____ play

_____

7. _____ fair

_____

8. _____ paint

_____

At Home: Put up a list on the refrigerator with two columns-one for words with the prefix *un* and the other for words with the prefix *re* . Everyone should add words as they think of them. Keep the list up for several days.

Book 3.1/Unit 1
Phoebe and the Spelling Bee

Steps in a Process

Make an upside-down face! You could draw the face of an animal, or draw a silly person. In the drawings above, a hairdo turns into a beard, a bow tie is also a hair bow, and a mouth becomes a wrinkle.

What steps must you follow to complete your upside-down face? Write them below your picture.

Book 3.1/Unit 1
Opt: An Illusionary Tale

At Home: Think of other activities you do at home and create a list of steps for each activity.

15

Vocabulary

length	within	straighten
royal	guard	gift

Write a paragraph about a royal castle, using as many vocabulary words from the box as you can. Then erase those vocabulary words or cover them with tape. Exchange paragraphs with a partner and fill in the blanks.

Story Comprehension

Opt is a land where things don't always look as they really are. As you answer each question, explain how you decided your answer.

1. Which line is longer—A or B? How can you prove you are correct?

2. Is the shape you see here a perfect circle? How can you prove you are correct? _____

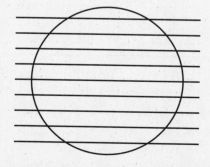

At Home: Students can draw their own characters who could live in Opt and label their drawings.

16–17

Book 3.1 / Unit 1
Opt: An Illusionary Tale

Use a Table of Contents

Here are the cover and table of contents page from the Opt Zoo brochure. Draw and color a picture that would make a good cover page. Then study the table of contents, and answer the questions below.

The Opt Zoo Brochure	Table of Contents
	Lions . . . . .Page 1 and Cage 1
	Tigers . . . . .Page 2 and Cage 2
	Bear, Oh My! . . .Page 3 and Cage 3
	Animals That Fly . . . . .Pages 4–6 and Cage 4

1. What animal would you visit first? _____

2. Suppose you wanted to start with the lions. You want to visit the animals in order. What animal would you visit after the lions?

_____

3. What pages talk about birds? How do you know? _____

_____

Write a story about your visit to this zoo.

_____

_____

_____

_____

Book 3.1 / Unit 1
Opt: An Illusionary Tale

At Home: Look through the newspaper together, and predict what the stories will be about by reading the headlines.

18

Steps in a Process

The following lists some things you might do if you are going to the zoo with the royal family. Two of these steps have nothing to do with going to the zoo. Mark an **X** beside those two steps. Then put the rest of the steps in order. Start with 1 for the first step. End with 5 for the last step.

Welcome to the Zoo
Kangaroos
→
this way

_____ **1.** Say goodbye to the royal family and go home.

_____ **2.** Look at a map to find out how to get to the king's castle.

_____ **3.** Tie a ribbon around your bike.

_____ **4.** Greet the royal family at the castle.

_____ **5.** Have lunch with the royal family after seeing all of the animals.

_____ **6.** Rearrange your bedroom furniture.

_____ **7.** With the king's help, look at a map to find the zoo.

At Home: Plan the steps for running an everyday errand.

Book 3.1 / Unit 1
Opt: An Illusionary Tale

McGraw-Hill School Division

Story Elements

A narrator tells a story. You can be a narrator. Or the narrator can be someone else who is telling a story from his or her point of view.
Read the statements about "Opt: An Illusionary Tale." Then answer each question.

Find the rod and find the branch of the tree. Now look at the Prince's shirt. What do you see?

1. Imagine the prince is telling the story from his point of view. How

would the second sentence be written? _____

_____

The guard marches up the stairs, but is he getting anywhere?

2. If the narrator told the story from the guard's point of view, how would

this sentence be written? _____

_____

The fire-breathing dragon now comes in. Turn the book and his eyes will spin. He arrives with presents and none too late. But did he tie the ribbons on straight?

3. Rewrite this paragraph from the dragon's point of view. _____

_____

_____

_____

Draw and color a picture of the dragon.

Book 3.1 / Unit 1
Opt: An Illusionary Tale

At Home: Suggest a favorite family story and try to tell it from a different narrator's point of view. Discuss how the point of view changes the story.

20

Prefixes

The prefixes di*s* and *un* can be added to some words to form their opposites. Read the sentences below. Add the prefix *un* or *dis* to a word in the first sentence to fill in the blank in the second sentence.

1. This is not your usual time. It is very _____ for you to be here now.

2. Do not agree with me! You must _____.

3. Flowers appear in the spring. They _____ when winter comes.

4. I was certain that I knew my words. However, now I'm really _____.

5. Muffin did not obey my signals. I'm disappointed when he _____.

6. That's not a real story. It is totally _____.

Imagine a visit to a museum or zoo. Use some words with the prefixes *dis* and *un* to tell a story about your imaginary visit.

_____

_____

_____

_____

_____

_____

At Home: Try to have a conversation using only words with no prefixes. Talk about how much we use prefixes to make ourselves clear.

Book 3.1 / Unit 1
Opt: An Illusionary Tale

21

McGraw-Hill School Division

Problem and Solution

Read the following story about Sarah. Then complete the Problem-Solution Chart to show how Sarah might solve her problem.

Sarah waited in the car for her mother. Sarah had an idea that she wanted to write in her journal before she forgot it. But it was too dark. Then she remembered she had some glow-in-the-dark ink pens in her backpack. Help Sarah solve her problem.

Sarah's Problem-Solution Chart

PROBLEM

What is the problem? _____

Who has the problem? _____

SOLUTION BOX

_____
_____
_____
_____

RESULT BOX

_____
_____
_____

McGraw-Hill School Division

At Home: Think of a problem a student might have, such as how to get homework finished on soccer-practice days. Write down possible solutions to the problem, and the result of each solution.

Vocabulary

ceiling	**cents**	**eager**
including	**scene**	**section**

Write each word in the box on a card. Write definitions for each word on other cards. Play a matching game with a partner. Place the word cards face down on one side and the definitions face down on another side. Turn over two cards at a time, one from each side. If the word matches the definition, keep the cards. If not, turn them over and let your partner have a turn.

Extend ◆ **24**

Story Comprehension

Imagine that you were at the sidewalk sale where Max and Gordy sold baseballs. On another sheet of paper, draw the sidewalk stands you would like to see there and label them. Put all the illustrations together into a booklet and gather them for the library corner. Or, organize your illustrations as a class and make one large book of sidewalk stands.

At Home: Look up entrepreneur together in the dictionary and discuss how Max and Gordy were entrepreneurs. Think of any other young people you know who are like Max.

23–24

Book 3.1/ Unit 1
Max Malone

Use an Index

Many books have an index. An index is at the back of the book. It lists specific information in the book and pages on which the information is located. Look at this part of an index. Then answer the questions below.

D	**E**
day, length, 21	eagles, 39
deserts, 90–91	ears, 82
dew, 68	parts, 83
digestion, 76	hearing, 85
dinosaurs, 27	Earth, 20
extinction, 28	earthquakes, 22
dogs, 53	earthworms, 25
ducks, 32	ecology, 69
	ecosystems, 70
	water, 71
	land, 73

1. Suppose you wanted to find a picture of an ear. What page would you check? _____

2. Some main topics have subtopics. Where would you read about water ecosystems? _____

3. On what page would you find out about how dinosaurs became extinct? _____

4. Under what main topic would you find information about hearing?

_____

5. Under what main topic would you find information about the living and nonliving things in a body of water?_____

Book 3.1/Unit 1
Max Malone

At Home: Go through indexes of books at home. Point out any differences you find.

25

McGraw-Hill School Division

Problem and Solution

There are solutions for most problems. Max and Gordy showed how to solve some problems. They also showed how to treat a good friend.

Suppose your school needs sports equipment. What ways can you think of to raise the money for your school to buy the equipment it needs?

_____

_____

_____

_____

_____

_____

_____

_____

_____

_____

_____

_____

_____

_____

_____

At Home: Talk about daily problem/solution situations that students regularly face and deal with. Help them to see where they are adept at coming up with solutions and where they may need more practice.

Book 3.1 / Unit 1
Max Malone

26

Story Elements

Complete the story map below. Tell what event in the story happened as a result of how the character felt. Under the character's name, draw a picture of the character's face showing how he felt.

CHARACTER	Character's Feelings	Story Event
Gordy	He wanted to start selling the baseballs.	_____ _____ _____ _____ _____
Max	Max had forgotten all about Austin.	_____ _____ _____ _____ _____ _____
Austin	Austin felt disappointed because he could not go to the sporting goods store to get Dusty's autograph.	_____ _____ _____ _____ _____

McGraw-Hill School Division

At Home: Ask students to draw a character they have read about, but have never seen in an illustration or on TV. Draw some conclusion about how easily readers picture their characters through the words they read.

27

Compound Words

every	mid	base	air	balls
thing	them	selves	one	

Use the words in the box to make compound words you can use in the sentences below.

1. The outfielder caught the fly ball in _____.

2. Max and Gordy bought forty-six _____.

3. They wanted signatures for _____ , too.

4. In the end, _____ was happy.

Use some of the compound words that you built to write a story.

_____

_____

_____

_____

_____

_____

_____

_____

_____

_____

At Home: Ask students to look at a newspaper for more compound words.

Book 3.1 / Unit 1
Max Malone

28

McGraw-Hill School Division

Make Predictions

Often you predict, or guess what will happen next, in something you read. Sometimes your predictions are correct and sometimes they are not. Read each passage below, then stop and predict what will happen next by answering the question that follows.

How do you know what's up and what's down?
What is it that keeps you from floating around?

1. Do you predict that this will be a poem, a riddle, a story, or an informative article? Explain. _____

_____

What do you think the answer might be?
The answer is simple . . . it's gravity.

2. Did these two lines make you change your prediction? _____

_____

Everything has gravity. An apple and a dog have gravity. You have gravity. Gravity pulls at everything on Earth, and everything on Earth pulls back.

3. Is your prediction still the same? Now what do you believe will come next?

_____

_____

Everything on Earth is pulled toward the center of the Earth. That is why Earth's gravity holds apples, dogs, you, and even air, water, and rocks down. Without gravity we would have no air to breathe or water to drink. Could we survive?

4. Does this passage confirm your latest prediction? Can you answer the last question in the passage? _____

_____

McGraw-Hill School Division

At Home: Go back over this exercise with students to see that the predictions were made through understanding of the text, not just wild guesses.

OUACHITA TECHNICAL COLLEGE

Vocabulary

Sometimes compound words make up new words. Think about words such as *downpour, paperback,* or *cattail.* Be creative with the words in the box to make compound words. Write your compound word in a sentence. See the examples.

celebrated	cork	fans	pitcher	score	wrap

1. _____ like to be near bulletin boards.

2. Halloween is a _____ holiday.

3. _____

4. _____

Story Comprehension

Work like an inventor. Follow steps to make something.

1. Read the list of materials below. Decide which materials you could use to make a tool for sending a message.

   electric wire   paper clips   mirror

   light bulb   paper   string

   battery   pen   paper cups

2. What are you making?

3. Decide your steps in creating your invention.

4. Draw a picture of what you made.

At Home: Talk about what goes into having ideas for inventions. It requires some wondering about how things work. Walk around, listing your home things that could be improved by a new invention.

30–31

Book 3.1/Unit 1
Champions of the World

McGraw-Hill School Division

Use a Search Engine

A computer catalog in a library lists all of the books in the library. A computer search can find books by subject, by title, and by author.

The left column below lists what you know about a book. In the right column write **author, title,** or **subject** to show which kind of search you would have the computer catalog perform.

What You Are Looking For

A book about baseball _____

A book by Allen Say _____

A book titled *Max Malone Makes a Million* _____

A book by Charlotte Herman _____

A book about optical illusions _____

A book about Sammy Sosa or Mark McGwire _____

A book titled *Grandfather's Journey* _____

Book 3.1 / Unit 1
Champions of the World

At Home: Discuss with students the different ways of searching for information in our computer age.

32

Steps in a Process

In "Champions of the World," you read about how to make a baseball.

Think about how you would make your own sports card.

Choose the size of card or paper you want to use.

Decide on the sport you want to be good at.

Draw a picture of yourself playing this sport.

Add color to the picture.

Decide on the information that belongs on the back.

List your name, where you were born, and the year.

List all the other important information.

What other finishing touches do you want to add?

Share the sports cards with classmates.

At Home: Look through a newspaper to find pictures or statistics on favorite sports figures.

Book 3.1/Unit 1
Champions of the World

33

Compound Words

In each sentence, there are two words that you can put together to make a compound word listed in the Word Box. Write the compound word on the line.

overhead	basketball	baseball	afternoon
airplane	grandfather	something	sunshine

1. The plane flew over my head. _____

2. The plane is in the air. _____

3. Please meet me at noon or after. _____

4. The waves seem to shine in the sun. _____

5. The ball went in the basket. _____

6. Some days I can't think of a thing to do. _____

7. Juan's father plays a grand piano. _____

8. The ball just missed me at first base. _____

At Home: Make a word box together of items in the room that can be put together to make a compound word.

Prefixes

A **prefix** is a word part that can be added to the beginning of a word to change the word's meaning. Knowing what a prefix means can help you figure out what a word means. The prefixes *un-* and *dis-* both mean "not" or "the opposite of."

Prefix	Means		
dis-	opposite of, not	**dis**appear	means "the opposite of appear"
un-	not, opposite of	**un**fair	means "not fair"

In each sentence, choose either the prefix **dis-** or **un-** for each of the underlined words, making new words with the opposite meanings. Rewrite each sentence by correctly using the new words.

1. I took my time to neatly <u>wrap</u> the gift.

_____

2. My teacher was very <u>pleased</u> with my good behavior.

_____

3. Please <u>tie</u> your shoe so you don't trip.

_____

4. She should <u>continue</u> working until she is finished.

_____

5. The warm weather is <u>usual</u> for this time of year.

_____

At Home: Invent some new words by adding prefixes to everyday words. Discuss which of your words make sense and which do not.

Book 3.1 / Unit 1
Champions of the World

35

Vocabulary Review

Unscramble each word putting the letters in the order of the numbers.

1. e   e   c   s   a   t   r   d   t
    8   6   2   1   3   5   7   9   4

    __ __ __ __ __ __ __ __ __

2. g   s   n   e   i   t   h   r   a   t
    6   1   10   9   5   2   7   3   4   8

    __ __ __ __ __ __ __ __ __ __

3. r   c   c   t   r   o   e
    4   1   6   7   3   2   5

    __ __ __ __ __ __ __

4. s   b   e   a   r   s   a   m   r
    9   3   1   7   6   8   4   2   5

    __ __ __ __ __ __ __ __ __

5. g   i   i   c   n   l   n   u   d
    9   1   7   3   2   4   8   5   6

    __ __ __ __ __ __ __ __ __

Write a paragraph including all the words you unscrambled.

_____

_____

_____

_____

_____

McGraw-Hill School Division

At Home: Have children cut out magazine pictures that illustrate the following words: **journey, surrounded, unusual, towering.** Have them scramble the letters in the word and give clues, along with the picture, to help a friend unscramble the word.

Vocabulary Review

Read the sentences. Then circle TRUE or FALSE. Then make the
FALSE statements TRUE.

1. When you are hungry, you are **eager** to eat.   TRUE   FALSE

_____

2. We walk on the **ceiling.**   TRUE   FALSE

_____

3. The teams' **scores** were red and blue uniforms.   TRUE   FALSE

_____

4. We felt safe because the dog was keeping **guard** of our house.

   TRUE   FALSE

_____

5. The car is so **enormous** that only four of us could fit and we had to

   leave the boxes behind.   TRUE   FALSE

_____

_____

6. We **celebrated** her birthday with cake and gifts.   TRUE   FALSE

_____

7. I was **astonished** to open a book and find words to read.

   TRUE   FALSE

_____

_____

At Home: Write each of the words on a separate card: **length, continue,
within, cents, fans,** and **wrap.** Pick a card and use this word in a TRUE or
FALSE sentence. Ask someone to guess if it is TRUE or FALSE.

Book 3.1 / Unit 1

McGraw-Hill School Division

Use a Telephone Directory

Bennet & Co. 10 3rd Street	555.8835	Hammar O. M. 11 3rd Street	555-1323
Bennett Sam 101 Broad Street	555-3497	Hammer's Supplies 29 3rd Street	555-6574
Bennett's Cakes 32 3rd Street	555-1483	Hammor's Pet Shop 2 3rd Street	555-9032

Suppose you live on 3rd Street. You want to get a group of 3rd Street business owners together to sponsor clean-up of the local park. You know the last names of the business owners. You don't have their telephone numbers. Here are the names of the business people you want to call. List the correct telephone numbers for these people. Then, tell how you found the correct number.

1. Mr. Hammer ———————————————

How did you decide his telephone number?

_____

_____

2. Mr. Bennett ———————————————

How did you decide his telephone number?

_____

_____

Describe what you will do to clean up the park.

_____

_____

_____

_____

McGraw-Hill School Division

At Home: Have students use the local telephone directory to look up three businesses. Have them list the businesses' names in alphabetical order followed by their numbers.

Cause and Effect

It is important to understand why events happen and what effect, or action, each event caused. The following are some events. Write what might have caused the event on the lines at the left. Write what might happen as a result of the event on the lines at the right.

Cause	**Event**	**Effect**
1. _____	Jo had an 11th	_____
_____	birthday party.	_____
_____		_____
2. _____	Moira and Chloe arrived	_____
_____	at the party together.	_____
_____		_____

Write a story about what you think happened at Jo's party.

_____

_____

_____

_____

_____

At Home: Have students write what else might have happened at Jo's party. Ask them to write a cause and effect for each event.

42

Book 3.1/Unit 2
City Green

Draw Conclusions

You should draw a conclusion based on information you know from your own experience or from information you research. Read each problem below. Then find out more about the problem. Ask a teacher or family member, look in library books, or use a computer to search for more information. Then write your conclusion. Give reasons for your conclusion.

1. Many buildings are getting very old. Should they be torn down? Should they be fixed up? Why do you think as you do?

_____

_____

_____

_____

2. Many areas are covered with litter and garbage. Should we help clean those areas up? Is that someone else's problem? Why do you think as you do?

_____

_____

_____

_____

At Home: Have students discuss what they think should be done to solve one of the problems.

Context Clues

It's not always easy to figure out what a word means. But if you look at all the other words and the pictures around them, sometimes you can figure it out. Read the sentence below each picture. Then, figure out what the underlined word means. Tell how you figured it out.

Why is that bird making such a hullabaloo?

Don't you think that horse is exquisite?

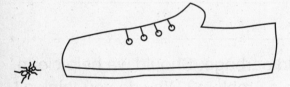

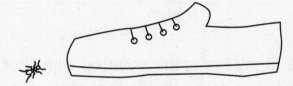

Look at that infinitesimal insect.

Yes, but the shoe looks colossal next to the ant.

Circle the correct meaning. Then tell how you learned the meaning.

1. Hullabaloo means loud noise or nest.

_____

2. Exquisite means running fast or pretty.

_____

3. Infinitesimal means very large or very tiny.

_____

4. Colossal means very tiny or very large.

_____

At Home: Have students use each of the new words to write a sentence.

McGraw-Hill School Division

Compare and Contrast

You can use a Venn diagram to compare and contrast two things. Write all the things that are true about both animals in the center. Write what is true about the bear only on the left. Write what is true about the bird only on the right.

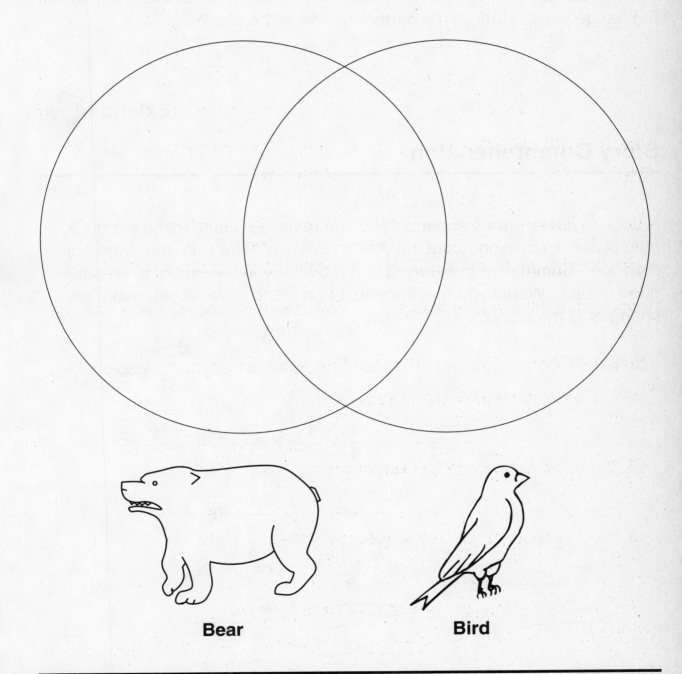

Bear   **Bird**

At Home: Have students pick two of their favorite toys or books. Challenge them to compare and contrast the toys or books using a Venn diagram.

Vocabulary

| canyons | flowed | grains | handful | peaks | traded |

Write a paragraph about nature. Use as many vocabulary words from the box as you can. Then erase the vocabulary words or cover them with tape. Exchange paragraphs with a partner and fill in the blanks.

Extend 47

Story Comprehension

A book reviewer writes about books. The reviewer summarizes the book, then states an opinion about it. Write a review of "The Sun, the Wind and the Rain." Summarize the story. Then tell what you thought of it. Was it good or bad? Would you recommend it to a friend? Would you make any changes to the story?

At Home: Ask students to describe Elizabeth's mountain and include what it looks like, how she built it, and where it is.

46–47

Book 3.1/Unit 2
The Sun, the Wind and the Rain

Use a Dictionary

Here are some words to define. Write a list of the steps you will take to find the word in the dictionary. Then define each word and use it in a sentence.

Step 1. _____

Step 2. _____

Step 3. _____

1. pebble _____

_____

2. loosen _____

_____

3. breeze _____

_____

4. tumble _____

_____

5. jagged _____

_____

6. sandstone _____

_____

Book 3.1/Unit 2
The Sun, the Wind and the Rain

At Home: Have students show you how to look up a word in the dictionary.

48

Compare and Contrast

Think about how animals and plants are alike and different. Fill out the chart to compare a pine tree and an owl.

Alike   **Different**

1. _____   4. _____

   _____   _____

   _____   _____

2. _____   5. _____

   _____   _____

   _____   _____

3. _____   6. _____

   _____   _____

   _____   _____

7. What might you title this table?

_____

At Home: Have students write a paragraph about the owl and the pine tree using the information they listed in the compare and contrast chart.

49

Book 3.1/Unit 2
The Sun, the Wind and the Rain

McGraw-Hill School Division

Draw Conclusions

Telephone Tale

Sometimes when people pass information from person to person, the information can change. See what will happen with a story you start.

Get together with a group of your classmates. You are the story starter. Make up a story about an animal. It may be a story about a pet monkey that gets loose and into trouble. Write your story on paper so that you can compare it to the story the group ends up with.

Have your group sit together. Tell your story quietly to the person next to you. When you are done, ask him or her to pass the story on to the next person. Ask the last person who hears the story to write it down on a piece of paper.

As a group, compare the two stories. Under the columns below, list how the stories were the same. List how the stories were different.

Similarities	**Differences**
_____	_____
_____	_____
_____	_____
_____	_____

What conclusions can you draw from this "telephone tale"?

_____

_____

McGraw-Hill School Division

Book 3.1/Unit 2
The Sun, the Wind and the Rain

At Home: Have students continue the telephone tale they started in their group.

50

Antonyms and Synonyms

Antonyms are words that have opposite meanings. Synonyms are words
that have the same or similar meanings. Read the words in the first box.
Write an antonym for each word.

rough	hard	dry	light	small

Antonyms

1. smooth _____ **4.** heavy _____

2. soft _____ **5.** big _____

3. wet _____

Look at the words in the second box. Write a synonym for each word.

wind	rush	hairy	sharp-edged	help

Synonyms

6. breeze _____ **9.** jagged _____

7. hurry _____ **10.** aid _____

8. furry _____

Look at the picture.
Use some of the words
in the boxes to write about it.

McGraw-Hill School Division

Cause and Effect

Look at the pictures below. Each one shows a cause. Write a story about each picture that gives a possible effect.

_____

_____

_____

_____

_____

_____

_____

_____

_____

At Home: Have students read their stories. Ask them to think of another way each story could end. Have them write a new ending showing the new effect.

Vocabulary

Write clues for the words in the crossword puzzle.

Across

1. _____

_____

3. _____

_____

5. _____

_____

6. _____

_____

Down

2. _____

_____

4. _____

_____

Story Comprehension

Decide if Tiblo and Tanksi ever meet the wolf again. Write and illustrate a story about what you think happened after the wolf left. Tell about the next adventure that you think Tiblo and Tanksi had.

At Home: Ask students if they have heard other stories about animals who have helped people. What were they about?

McGraw-Hill School Division

Use an Encyclopedia

You and your family are on the way to pick berries to make pies and cakes. You want to make sure you get berries that will be sweet and tasty. You also want to make sure that any berries you pick can be used in food.

Here are some different kinds of berries you could pick. Describe how you would find out about each one in an encyclopedia. Then pick one of these berries to research in your school library's encyclopedia. Write what you find out on another piece of paper.

boysenberry

elderberry

strawberry

blackberry

raspberry

Let's Go Berry-Picking

_____

_____

_____

_____

_____

_____

_____

_____

McGraw-Hill School Division

Cause and Effect

Many things happen in the fall as the temperature changes. No matter where you live, the change in temperature and amount of sun cause things to happen. Describe some of the effects that fall causes where you live.

1. About what time does the sun set at the beginning of August where

   you live? _____

   About what time does the sun set at the beginning of October?

   _____

2. Describe some effects that the change in temperature and the amount of sunlight has on plants where you live.

   _____

   _____

   _____

3. Describe some effects that fall has on animals where you live.

   _____

   _____

   _____

4. Write a paragraph that tells what happens in the fall to plants, animals, and you.

   _____

   _____

   _____

   _____

   _____

   _____

At Home: Have students describe what happens to the plants where they live between October and January.

Book 3.1/Unit 2
Dream Wolf

56

McGraw-Hill School Division

Compare and Contrast

Different places have different kinds of weather, but most places have four seasons. In the center of the web below write how the four seasons are alike where you live. In each of the four outer circles write how each season is different.

At Home: Have students write two sentences about each season, describing what is the same and what is different about each.

Context Clues

Read the underlined words and look at the pictures. Decide what each word means. Then write another sentence using the same word.

1. The wolf is sleeping in its warm <u>den</u>.

_____

2. Another name for buffalo is <u>bison</u>.

_____

3. These animals are not dogs. They are <u>prairie dogs</u>.

_____

Use at least one of the underlined words to write a poem.

_____

_____

_____

_____

At Home: Have children select one of the words. Ask them to write and illustrate a story using the word they chose.

Book 3.1/Unit 2
Dream Wolf

58

Important and Unimportant Information

When you look for information, ask yourself: What questions do I want to answer? Knowing what your questions are will tell you which information is important.

Read the list of subjects below. Underline the question you might want to ask about each one.

Subject	Questions
1. lizards	What are different kinds of lizards?
2. the year 2050	What is an endangered plant?
3. endangered	How old will I be in the year 2050?
4. horses	What happened in 1923?
	How can I help endangered animals?
	How fast can horses run?
	Do lizards eat lettuce?

Think of two subjects. Write questions you would like answered about each one.

My subjects

5. _____

6. _____

My questions

_____

_____

_____

_____

Book 3.1/Unit 2
Spiders at Work

At Home: Have students choose a subject from the list and research it.

59

McGraw-Hill School Division

Vocabulary

| capture | liquid | ruin | serious | skills | struggles |

Concentration Game

Write each vocabulary word on a different card. Write the definitions on other cards. Place the cards face down. Play a matching game with a partner. Turn over two cards at a time. If the word matches the definition, keep both cards and play again. If the cards don't match, turn them both over and let your partner have a turn.

Story Comprehension

What did you find out about spiders? Write and illustrate a booklet about spiders. Include the most interesting facts from "Spiders at Work." Then share the booklet with your class.

At Home: Have students use some of the words in the box to write some facts about spiders.

Book 3.1/Unit 2
Spiders at Work

60–61

Use a Dictionary

A. Use a dictionary. Find out what each word means.

1. dangerous _____

_____

2. allergy _____

_____

3. sting _____

_____

4. tarantula _____

_____

B. Use the words to write a story about Ned the tarantula.

_____

_____

_____

_____

_____

_____

_____

Book 3.1/Unit 2
Spiders at Work

At Home: Have students write as many sentences as they can using the word **sting** in different ways.

62

Important and Unimportant Information

We draw. We write. We talk. Sometimes we sign. We do these activities to communicate. When you communicate directions or instructions, you need to make sure you communicate what is most important.

Write how to make a peanut butter and jelly sandwich. Make sure you write exactly what to do. Keep it simple.

_____

_____

_____

_____

_____

Ask a friend or family member to follow your instructions and make a peanut butter and jelly sandwich.

Now tell someone how to make a peanut butter and jelly sandwich by speaking. You can use gestures. Compare the two sandwiches. Explain why one looks better than the other.

Write down any of the information in your directions that was unimportant.

_____

_____

Explain how you could do a better job of telling or writing how to make the sandwich.

_____

_____

At Home: Have students tell how to make another kind of sandwich they like to eat. Remind them to include only the important steps.

Book 3.1/Unit 2
Spiders at Work

63

McGraw-Hill School Division

Draw Conclusions

A conclusion is what you decide to think about something based on what you see, what you already know, and on any other information you have. Look at each of the pictures below. Draw a conclusion about what is happening in each one.

1.
_____
_____
_____
_____

2.
_____
_____
_____
_____

3.
_____
_____
_____
_____

Choose one picture. Write a story about it on another piece of paper.

At Home: Have students write another scenario for what might be happening in each picture.

Antonyms and Synonyms

Antonyms are words that have opposite meanings. Synonyms are words that have the same or similar meanings. Read the story.

The <u>helpful</u> spider took a fly to her <u>ill</u> friend. The friend was <u>grateful</u> for a chance to <u>eat</u>. She took the fly and ate it <u>quickly</u>.

"Thank you," she said. "You are a true <u>friend</u>."

A. Rewrite the story using **synonyms** for the underlined words.

The _____ spider took a fly to her _____ friend.

The friend was _____ for a chance to _____ . She

took the fly and ate it _____ .

"Thank you," she said. "You are a true _____ ."

B. Rewrite the story using **antonyms** for the underlined words.

The _____ spider took a fly to her _____ friend.

The friend was _____ for a chance to _____ . She

took the fly and ate it _____ .

"Thank you," she said. "You are a true _____ ."

C. How did using synonyms affect the story? What happened when you used antonyms?

_____

_____

_____

_____

At Home: Have students use antonyms to write pairs of sentences with opposite meanings.

Book 3.1/Unit 2
Spiders at Work

65

Compare and Contrast

Knowing what is true and what is not true helps you compare correctly.
Read the statements about plants and animals below. Write **Yes** beside the
ones that are true. Write **No** beside the ones that are not true. Then use the
Venn diagram to compare and contrast plants and animals.

1. Both plants and animals are living things._____

2. Some animals eat plants, but most plants make their own food.

_____

3. Plants can move from place to place. _____

4. Animals can fly, walk, or swim. _____

5. There are many different kinds of plants and animals.

_____

6. Plants do not need water, but animals do. _____

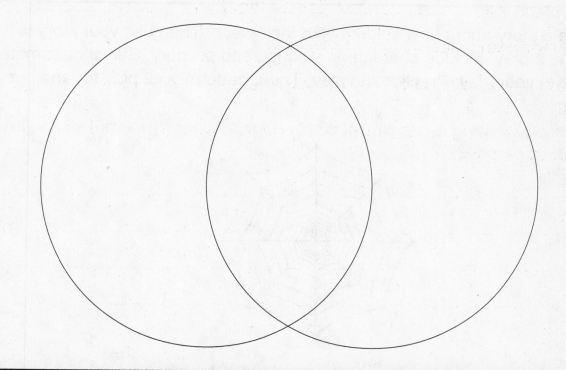

At Home: Have students use the information listed in the
diagram to write a paragraph comparing plants and
animals.

Vocabulary

crops	earthquake	hatch	respect	soldiers	woven

Make up a tall tale with a partner. First list five things that will happen in your make-believe story. Use as many of the words in the box as you can to write your tale. Invite younger students to a story hour. Before they arrive, practice reading your story aloud. Change you voice to fit the characters in the story.

Extend 68

Story Comprehension

Write a story about how spiders spin their webs. Then use your story to create a play. Include characters, a script, and scenery. Select classmates to be in your play. Practice the play. Then, perform your play for another class.

At Home: Have students discuss other famous fairy tales they know well. List the characters together and the important details in the stories.

67–68

Book 3.1/Unit 2
Web Wonders

McGraw-Hill School Division

Use a Resource

There are many different places you can find information. When you need a definition of a word you can look in a dictionary. When you need to know where a country is, you can look on a map. When you want to learn about a topic, you can use an encyclopedia or search the Internet on a computer.

Read the questions below. Write the resource or resources that could give you the information you need to answer the question. It may be a dictionary, a map, an encyclopedia, or the Internet.

1. What does *hatch* mean? _____

2. Is a tarantula an arachnid that spins a web? _____

3. Where is South America? _____

4. How do spiders spin strong webs? _____

5. How far can the wind carry baby spiders? _____

Choose two questions to answer. Use a resource. Write the answers below.

_____

_____

_____

_____

_____

_____

_____

_____

Book 3.1/Unit 2
Web Wonders

At Home: Have students use a resource to find out more about a topic of their own choice.

69

Important and Unimportant Information

A. Suppose you are planning a hike in the mountains. There is some important information you will need to know. Read the questions below. Decide which information is important for your hike. Write the word **important** beside the three questions you need to find the answers to.

1. What equipment should you take on a hike?

_____

2. What should you do if you see a bear in the mountains?

_____

3. What shoes work best for running? _____

4. What snacks and drinks should you take on a hike?

_____

5. What equipment do skiers use? _____

B. Find out the answer to each important question. Write a paragraph that explains what is important for going on a hike.

Planning a Hike

_____

_____

_____

_____

_____

_____

At Home: Have students use the important information to draw a picture of someone who is hiking safely.

Book 3.1/Unit 2
Web Wonders

70

Antonyms and Synonyms

A. Synonyms are words that have similar meanings. Read about some inventions that never made it. Then find a synonym in the box that you can use for the underlined words in the paragraphs.

destroyed	live	hoped	earth	sail	person

Inventions That Never Got Off the Ground

In 1869, Leopold Trouvvelot tried to get caterpillars and silkworms to reproduce. He <u>wished</u> ————————— to produce caterpillars that could <u>reside</u> ————————— in American trees and spin silk. His experiment didn't work, but his caterpillars got loose and <u>killed</u> ————————— a lot of trees.

In 1961, a "Rocket Belt" was invented. A <u>human</u> ————————— wearing it could <u>fly</u> ————————— 80 feet off the <u>ground</u> ————————— at 6 miles an hour. The problem was that there was only enough fuel for 21 minutes.

B. Antonyms are words with opposite meanings. Choose four words from the paragraphs above. Write an antonym for each word.

1. _____

2. _____

3. _____

4. _____

At Home: Challenge students to find as many other synonyms for the words in the box as they can.

McGraw-Hill School Division

Context Clues

A. The underlined words in the sentences below are scrambled. Look at the picture and read the sentences to figure out what the words should be. Write the correct word next to the scrambled word.

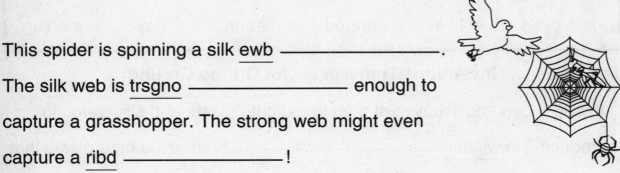

This spider is spinning a silk <u>ewb</u> ——————————.

The silk web is <u>trsgno</u> ——————————— enough to

capture a grasshopper. The strong web might even

capture a <u>ribd</u> ——————————!

B. Draw your own picture. Write sentences about it. Include three scrambled words. Give your picture and sentences to a partner. Ask your partner to unscramble the words.

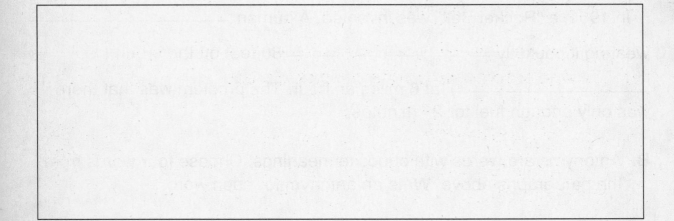

_____

_____

_____

_____

At Home: Invite students to read a passage in a story. Encourage them to use context clues to figure out the meaning of any unfamiliar words.

Book 3.1/Unit 2
Web Wonders

72

McGraw-Hill School Division

Name________________________________ Date____________ **Extend** 73

Vocabulary Review

Read each word. Use the word to write a sentence about the picture. Or draw a picture to illustrate the sentence.

1. **buffalo**

____

2. Tom poured **liquid** into a glass to drink.

3. **flowed**

____

4. The **ripe** peaches were perfect to pick and eat.

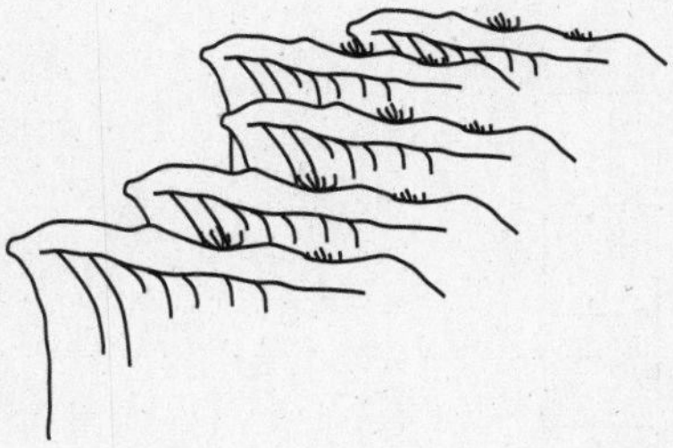

5. **canyons**

____

6. The marching **soldier** is very proud and brave.

At Home: Have students make a picture dictionary. On each page they can write a sentence for **darkness, peaks, stems, heap** and the bold words above. Then have them illustrate some of the words in their dictionaries.

Vocabulary Review

Use the words in the puzzle.

area excitement echoes earthquake darkness
shelter heap skills peaks respect

Across

1. We were filled with —————— as the party began.

3. Jan turned off the light so she could sleep in ——————.

5. We raked the leaves in a big —————— and jumped in it.

6. We learned addition —————— in first grade.

7. It was a large —————— in which to pitch our tent.

8. I have much —————— for my teacher and her knowledge.

9. The mountain —————— were covered in snow.

Down

1. We heard —————— when we shouted down into the canyon.

2. The —————— made the land shake and crack.

4. It began to rain so we ran into a cave for ——————.

At Home: Have children write their own clues for halfway, handful, traded, serious, struggles, capture and woven.

Main Idea

Read the story. Use the information to write a main-idea statement.

Matthew is too excited to sleep tonight. He is thinking about what will happen tomorrow when he wakes up. Early in the morning the whole family will drive to the airport to pick up Grandma and Grandpa. Aunt Lisa will arrive around lunchtime. After lunch everyone will go to the high school where Matthew will compete in his town's debating contest.

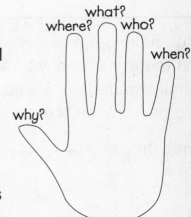

Mom comes in with a book and sits on Matthew's bed. They take turns reading pages from one of his favorite books. Matthew starts jumping on the bed. Mom tells him that she knows he is excited but he should just relax and listen. He asks for a drink of water. Mom brings him a glass of water and puts it on his dresser next to his bed. He reaches over and takes a sip of the water.

Mom tells Matthew that he can count sheep. Even after counting fifty sheep, he still can't sleep.

It is almost ten o'clock. Mom starts to hum a lullaby that she sang to Matthew when he was small. The music sounds soft and special to him. The melody is the last thing he remembers before falling asleep.

Now write your main-idea statement.

_____

_____

Write about a time you were so excited that you couldn't sleep.

_____

_____

_____

_____

McGraw-Hill School Division

Book 3.1/Unit 3
Moses Goes to a Concert

At Home: Have students repeat the activity with other favorite stories.

75

Vocabulary

concert	instrument	musician	conductor	orchestra	ill

You have been asked to take part in a special musical performance. Write the name of your instrument and draw its picture. Write to a family member or friend on another piece of paper. Use as many words from the box as you can to invite them to your performance.

Instrument _____

Story Comprehension

Work with a group to write a scene from "Moses Goes to a Concert." Choose actors. Have them use spoken words and sign language to play their parts. Present your scene to the class.

At Home: Have students invent another character for the story "Moses Goes to a Concert" and prepare dialogue for the new character.

76–77

Book 3.1/Unit 3
Moses Goes to a Concert

Use a Diagram

Moses and the other children at his school communicate by using American Sign Language. In this language, a sign can stand for a letter of the alphabet, a whole word, or even an idea. The diagram below shows the hand signs for letters in American Sign Language. This alphabet is important because for some words, such as names, there are no signs.

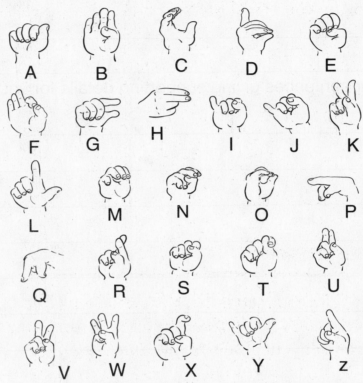

With a partner, practice signing the letters of the finger spelling alphabet. Take turns signing a letter. Ask your partner to tell what letter you are signing.

After you have practiced using each letter, challenge each other by finger spelling names of towns and cities in your state, and names of classmates.

Write a sentence telling why it is important to finger spell all the letters in a name correctly.

_____

_____

McGraw-Hill School Division

Book 3.1/Unit 3
Moses Goes to a Concert

At Home: Have students refer to the diagram as they practice finger spelling names of objects. Invite them to make a glossary showing the hand sign and written word of each word they can "say" with the finger-spelling alphabet.

Main Idea

Write a main-idea sentence for "Moses Goes to a Concert."

_____

_____

Develop an idea for another story about Moses and his friends. Write a main idea sentence for this story.

_____

_____

Write three or four sentences giving supporting details for your story.

_____

_____

_____

_____

_____

_____

_____

_____

_____

_____

_____

_____

_____

_____

McGraw-Hill School Division

At Home: Have students draw a picture illustrating the main-idea sentence for their original story.

Summarize

Read the paragraphs about the planet Earth.

The planet earth is the only planet in the solar system with large amounts of water on its surface and in its atmosphere. Earth is the third planet from the sun. The water in the oceans would boil away if the sun were much closer. If the earth were farther away from the sun, the water would turn to ice. The sun is just the right distance away.

Earth is larger than Mercury, Mars, Venus, and Pluto but smaller than all of the other planets. From space earth looks like a perfectly round ball, but it is really wider in the middle than at the top and bottom.

Earth is tilted a little to one side as it travels around the sun. As it goes around the sun, it spins like a big top. Each spin takes about twenty-four hours and is called a day.

A blanket of air circles the earth to keep the temperature from changing too much. This blanket of air is called the atmosphere. The people on the planet Earth live at the bottom of the atmosphere.

Write a paragraph summarizing the information about planet Earth.
Be sure to include important information from each of the paragraphs.

_____

_____

_____

_____

_____

Book 3.1/Unit 3
Moses Goes to a Concert

At Home: Have students draw pictures to summarize the paragraphs about planet Earth.

80

Context Clues

Use the words in the box to complete the story.

conductor	orchestra	marimba	kettledrum
snare drum	percussion	cymbal	triangle

Our class went to hear a concert performed by our town's

_____. The musicians knew exactly when they were supposed to

play. The _____ stood in front of them with his baton in his hand,

and directed their playing. There were many different _____

instruments that were played by being hit or shaken. There were several

kinds of drums, including a small double-headed drum called a

_____ because of the snares across its lower head. It made a

sound like a rattle when it was played. I liked the drum that looked like a

giant covered soup bowl. It is called a _____ .

There were other instruments, too. One of my favorites, the _____

looked a little like a piano keyboard, but you play it with sticks and not your

fingers. The brass _____ is shaped like a plate, but I can't imagine

eating my dinner on it! To play it you strike it with a stick or even with

another instrument just like it. I think the steel _____ has the

funniest name of all. It makes me think of shapes we study in school.

At Home: Have students underline the context clues in the story that helped them fill in the correct word.

Book 3.1/Unit 3
Moses Goes to a Concert

81

McGraw-Hill School Division

Story Elements

Follow the directions to create a setting for a story of farm life.

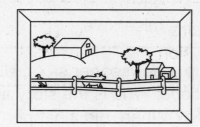

1. Place a sheet of paper over a large piece of coarse fabric, such as burlap, muslin, denim, terry cloth, or corduroy.

2. Use colored chalk or charcoal pencil to draw a farm scene on the paper. Be sure to include some people or animals in your drawing.

3. Separate your drawing from the fabric.

4. Write a title on your picture, and sign your name.

Use the lines below to write names for the people and animals in your drawing.

_____

_____

_____

Write a few sentences about the story's plot.

_____

_____

_____

Share your picture with the rest of the class. Tell about the setting, characters, and plot.

Book 3.1/Unit 3
**The Little Painter
of Sabana Grande**

At Home: Have students use their notes to write a farm story.

82

McGraw-Hill School Division

Vocabulary

blossoms	dawn	faded
imaginary	miserable	shallow

Work with a partner to make up a newspaper story. Use the words in the box to answer these questions: Who is the story about? What happened? When did it happen? Where did it happen? Why did it happen? Write your story on another piece of paper.

Story Comprehension

Write a new ending for "The Little Painter of Sabana Grande." Try to imagine what might have happened if Fernando had plenty of paper to paint on.

_____

_____

_____

_____

_____

_____

_____

At Home: Have students draw a picture of an adobe house painted by Fernando.

83–84

Book 3.1/Unit 3
The Little Painter of Sabana Grande

Use a Map

Work with a group to create a "picture map" of Panama and the rest of Central America. Find a large map of Central America. Trace the outline of Central America on a sheet of paper. Then think of things you can draw on your map to show important products, land features, plants, and animals. Take turns drawing the things you think of. Look at the real map to make sure you draw your pictures in the right places.

To find things to add to your map, have each member of the group research one of the countries in Central America. Look in books about Central America to find out about important products and other things you can add to your map. Display your picture map in the classroom for everyone to see.

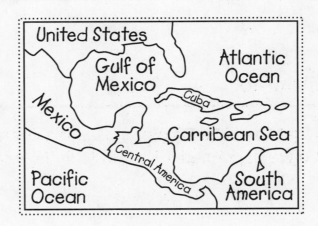

McGraw-Hill School Division

At Home: Have students write a paragraph describing the different plants and animals pictured on their map.

Story Elements

Imagine what it might be like to spend the day with Fernando, the main character in "The Little Painter of Sabana Grande." Write a paragraph telling about your imagined day.

_____

_____

_____

_____

Illustrate the setting of your imagined day with Fernando.

Share your paragraph and illustration with the rest of the class. Tell about the setting, characters, and plot.

McGraw-Hill School Division

At Home: Have students make up a simple plot for a story about something Fernando might do when he grows up.

Book 3.1/Unit 3
The Little Painter of Sabana Grande

Summarize

Make a list of the things you do during a day at your school. Use the list to write a letter to a friend summarizing what your school day is like. Tell only the important points. Include sentences describing the setting and the people at your school.

Dear _____,

_____

_____

_____

_____

_____

_____

_____

Your friend,

_____

At Home: Have students summarize a favorite story. Tell them to keep their summary to a few sentences.

Context Clues

Write a sentence telling the meaning of the word in dark type in each sentence.

Circle the words that helped you figure out the meaning.

1. There are only a few houses made of clay **adobe** in our small village.

_____

_____

2. At dinner, we fill our warm, fried, flour **tortillas** with meat and cheese.

_____

_____

Work with a partner to play Word Detective. Have each person make a list of four words. Write a sentence using context clues for each of the words. Draw a picture or cartoon with clues to illustrate the meaning of each word. Exchange sentences and pictures. Try to guess all the meanings of the words on your partner's list.

At Home: Have students draw a picture illustrating the meaning of the words *adobe* and *tortillas*.

88

Book 3.1/Unit 3
The Little Painter of Sabana Grande

McGraw-Hill School Division

Make Inferences

Read the story. Use story clues and what you already know to find out how Jenna feels about Anna's pet bird.

"This is my bird, Peppa," said Anna. "I'll let him out so you can hold him."

Jenna did not want Anna to let Peppa out. She said, "I can see that Peppa is a very beautiful bird. You don't have to let him out."

"Oh, but he is so sweet. You won't know how soft he feels if I don't let him out," said Anna.

Anna opened Peppa's cage and out he flew. First he landed on Anna's shoulder. She rubbed his neck and let him go. He flew in circles and then landed right on Jenna's arm.

Jenna didn't move. She let out a small scream.

"Jenna, he likes you!" cried Anna excitedly.

Jenna did not even answer her.

What clues in the text help you know how Jenna feels?

_____

_____

What do you know about people and pets that will help you know how Jenna feels?

_____

_____

What can you infer about how Jenna feels?

_____

_____

Book 3.1/Unit 3
The Patchwork Quilt

At Home: Have students make an inference about how Anna was feeling.

89

McGraw-Hill School Division

Vocabulary

anxious	attic	costume	examined	gazed	pattern

Make up a story with a partner. First make a list of the events that will happen in the story. Then use words in the box to tell how the characters feel or what they will do. Write your story on another piece of paper.

Story Comprehension

Work with a group to make a patchwork quilt "drawing" about your class that you "won't forget." Group members can include a drawing that tells something special about themselves. Write a sentence under each picture that tells what is important about it.

At Home: Have students write a paragraph about other ways besides quilting that families might use to record special memories.

90–91

Book 3.1/Unit 3
The Patchwork Quilt

McGraw-Hill School Division

Use a Diagram

Make your own quilt pattern. Use colored pencils or markers and the graph paper below to make a design for a quilt. Exchange patterns with a partner. Try creating a paper quilt. Use colored construction paper, scissors, and glue to create a paper quilt by following your partner's design.

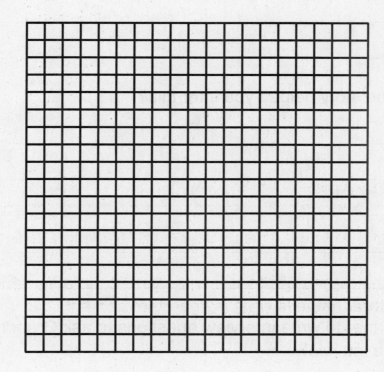

At Home: Have students make a pattern showing a design for a decorative screen or wall hanging.

Make Inferences

Write a sentence or two about "The Patchwork Quilt" telling how you think Grandma feels about the past.

_____

_____

_____

_____

What clues in the story helped you infer this?

_____

_____

_____

_____

Work with a partner to write interview questions to ask Grandma about her past. Act out the interview.

At Home: Have students write a sentence telling why they think Tanya removed a few squares from Grandma's old quilt.

Book 3.1/Unit 3
The Patchwork Quilt

93

Main Idea

Work with a group to read copies of a short newspaper article. Write a sentence stating the main idea of the article. List the supporting details from the article. List any details from the article that do not support the main idea.

MAIN IDEA:

_____

SUPPORTING DETAILS:

_____

_____

_____

_____

OTHER DETAILS:

_____

_____

Write a sentence telling why you think the article might have included details that do not support the main idea.

_____

_____

_____

Book 3.1/Unit 3
The Patchwork Quilt

At Home: Have students read a short magazine or newspaper article and identify the main idea and two supporting details.

94

Multiple-Meaning Words

Read each joke. Then write a sentence below the joke using the word in dark type.

1. Why is the river rich? Because it has two **banks.**

_____

_____

2. What did the elephant take on vacation? His **trunk.**

_____

_____

3. Why is a tall building like a book of fairy tales? It has lots of **stories.**

_____

_____

Write your own joke using any of the following multiple-meaning words: **cold, fresh, soft,** and **worn.**

_____

_____

At Home: Have students draw a picture illustrating two meanings for the word bank.

Book 3.1/Unit 3
The Patchwork Quilt

95

McGraw-Hill School Division

Story Elements

Complete the chart with information from your favorite fairy tale.

Title _____

Author _____

Setting _____

_____

Main Characters _____

_____

How did it begin? _____

_____

_____

_____

What happened in the middle? _____

_____

_____

_____

How did it end? _____

_____

_____

_____

At Home: Have students illustrate a cover for the story they described.

Vocabulary

combine	invented	located	prairie	stumbled	wilderness

Write a paragraph on another piece of paper telling about an adventure, using as many vocabulary words from the box as you can. Then erase those vocabulary words or cover them with tape. Exchange paragraphs with a partner and fill in the blanks.

Story Comprehension

Work with a partner to make up your own tall tales. Think of situations that might be difficult to get out of. Write one of these below. Take turns giving a tall tale response. Make your tales as tall as can be! When you are finished, choose your favorite tall tale and tell it to the rest of the class.

_____

_____

_____

At Home: Have students give a tall tale response to a question about why they were late for an imaginary appointment.

97–98

Book 3.1/Unit 3
Pecos Bill

McGraw-Hill School Division

Use a Map

Carl the Cowboy and Pecos Bill might have found a trail when they traveled home by using a map and map key. A map key has symbols to help you find things. Use the map and map key below to answer the questions.

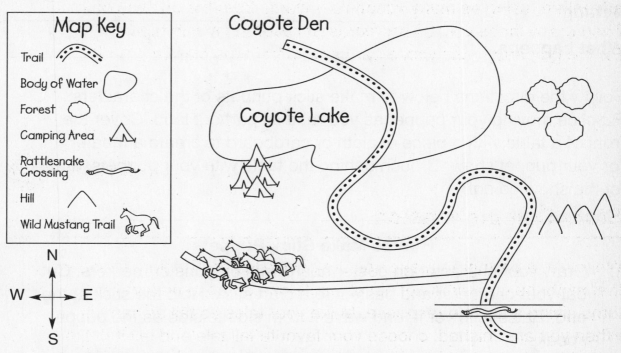

1. What direction will Carl and Pecos Bill travel to get to the forest?

_____

2. Is the forest east or west of Coyote Lake?

_____

3. Is the Rattlesnake Crossing closer to the hills or to Coyote Lake?

_____

Write a sentence telling something that you think Carl and Pecos Bill might have done while traveling along the trail.

_____

_____

McGraw-Hill School Division

Book 3.1/Unit 3
Pecos Bill

At Home: Have students use a map to show three states Pecos Bill might have crossed while chasing the wild mustang.

99

Story Elements

Work with a group to present a "Pecos Bill" puppet show for your class. Decide which scene you will show. Fill out the chart.

Characters: _____

Setting: _____

What happens: _____

Follow the directions below to make stick puppets of the characters. Practice moving your puppet as you read its part out loud. Cover the front of a table with a piece of cloth or cardboard to create a theater for your puppet show. Crouch behind the table with your puppets, and let the show go on!

How to Make Stick Puppets

Draw your character on poster board with crayons or markers. Cut out your character and paste it to a craft stick. Hold the stick at the end. Raise it, lower it, and wave it from side to side as the puppet speaks.

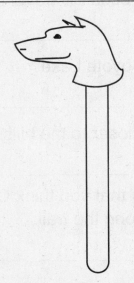

At Home: Have students write a sentence telling which event in the plot of "Pecos Bill" was the funniest or most exciting.

Book 3.1/Unit 3
Pecos Bill

100

McGraw-Hill School Division

Make Inferences

Play "Pass the Story" with a partner. Begin writing a story about anything you choose on the lines below.

_____

_____

_____

_____

_____

Exchange pages with your partner. Finish the story you receive on the lines below. Use clues from the story and what you already know to make inferences about how it should end.

_____

_____

_____

_____

_____

_____

Exchange pages again. Read what your partner wrote. Did he or she end the story the way you would have?

At Home: Read the first paragraph from a news story and have students write an ending to it.

McGraw-Hill School Division

Multiple-Meaning Words

| fix | story | right | pack | den | close |

Write a silly story with multiple-meaning words. Use each word from the word box twice. Be sure to use a different meaning of the word each time you use it. If you do not know multiple meanings for some of the words, you may use a dictionary for help. When you have finished, exchange stories with a partner. Tell the clues that helped you figure out the meaning of the multiple-meaning words used in your partner's story.

_____

_____

_____

_____

_____

_____

_____

_____

_____

At Home: Have students draw pictures to illustrate the multiple-meaning words *close* or *wind*. Challenge students to use them to create a tall tale.

Book 3.1/Unit 3
Pecos Bill

102

McGraw-Hill School Division

Main Idea

Write a paragraph about an interesting animal. Include a main idea sentence and supporting details. Write one sentence in the paragraph that does not support the main idea. Exchange paragraphs with a partner. Have your partner find the sentence that does not belong. Then have your partner suggest one more supporting sentence for the paragraph.

_____

_____

_____

_____

_____

_____

Draw a picture that shows the main idea of your paragraph.

McGraw-Hill School Division

At Home: Ask students to create new titles for a favorite story. Have them write a main-idea sentence for the story using one of the new titles.

Vocabulary

| beauty | creeps | furniture | palace | pure | visitors |

Write a paragraph about going to visit a castle. Use as many words from the box as you can to describe the people and the things that you see there.

Story Comprehension

Imagine that you are responsible for selling trips to the Ice Hotel. Work in a group to write advertisements and make posters for the Ice Hotel. Include information in your advertisements and posters that will make people want to visit. Write a slogan, or clever saying, about the Ice Hotel that you can use in your ads.

_____

_____

_____

_____

_____

_____

McGraw-Hill School Division

At Home: Have students write a sentence that might describe people who visit the Ice Hotel.

104–105

Book 3.1/Unit 3
A Very Cool Place to Visit

Use a Map

Each spring, the Ice Hotel melts. When the winter comes, the building of the Ice Hotel begins again. If the owners of the Ice Hotel plan to begin building a new hotel when the temperature is below 25 degrees, the information on a climate map can help them. Use the climate map on page 384 in your pupil edition to help the owners at the Ice Hotel make their plans.

Write a sentence telling the owners where they could build a new hotel during the month of January.

_____

_____

Which city might be the best location for building an ice hotel? Why?

_____

_____

McGraw-Hill School Division

At Home: Have students write a paragraph telling whether they would want to visit Sweden in January or July. Have them explain their answer.

Summarize

Review "A Very Cool Place to Visit." Write a short summary of the article in the space below. Then use the summary to write a television commercial that you might make telling people what a great place the Ice Hotel is to visit on vacation. Present your commercial to your classmates.

"A Very Cool Place to Visit" tells about _____

_____

_____

_____

_____

_____

_____

_____

_____

At Home: Have students write a paragraph summarizing a visit they have made or would like to make to a special place.

107

Book 3.1/Unit 3
A Very Cool Place to Visit

McGraw-Hill School Division

Multiple-Meaning Words

Read each sentence below. Use context clues in each sentence to define the meaning of each word in dark type. Circle the letter of the best meaning. Then, write sentences using the other meaning of each multiple-meaning word.

1. My friend lives on the same city **block** as I do.

   a. an area surrounded by four streets

   b. a piece of something hard

2. It is going to be a **cool** night at the park so Matt will bring a sweater.

   a. fashionable and trendy

   b. rather cold

3. The new student was given a **warm** welcome by the teacher and her classmates.

   a. a bit hot

   b. very friendly

4. When I stayed home from school with a **cold,** I sneezed and coughed all day.

   a. a common mild illness

   b. having a low temperature

1. _____

2. _____

3. _____

4. _____

Book 3.1/Unit 3
A Very Cool Place to Visit

At Home: Have students write a riddle for both meanings of the word bark.

108

Context Clues

Use the words in the box to complete the sentences.

snowsuit	sleeping bag	push-ups	reindeer	cube	sprinkle

1. It is a good idea to put on a heavy _____ before going outside to play on a cold winter day.

2. _____ a little brown sugar on your cereal to make it taste sweet.

3. There was plenty of room in the tent for me to roll out my _____ at bedtime.

4. Sometimes I think I would like to drive a sled pulled by _____ .

5. We warm up during gym class by doing sit-ups, _____ , and other exercises.

6. The drink was so warm in the hot sun that the _____ of ice melted right away.

Use all the words to write a paragraph telling what you might do on a visit to the Ice Hotel.

_____

_____

_____

_____

At Home: Have students draw picture clues for each word.

Book 3.1/Unit 3
A Very Cool Place to Visit

109

McGraw-Hill School Division

Vocabulary Review

Find each word in the box in the puzzle. Words may be written forward, backward, or down. Circle the words in the puzzle. Put the letters you did not circle in the spaces in the order you find them. Then answer the question.

anxious	invented	dawn	pattern	pure	prairie	gazed
palace	creeps	stumbled	ill	instrument	combine	blossom

```
p  r  a  i  r  i  e  s  w  i  p
a  n  x  i  o  u  s  t  l  d  a
l  c  r  e  e  p  s  u  e  r  t
a  i  n  s  t  r  u  m  e  n  t
c  l  n  e  c  o  m  b  i  n  e
e  l  m  o  s  s  o  l  b  s  r
p  u  r  e  g  a  z  e  d  s  n
i  n  v  e  n  t  e  d  a  w  n
```

Describe what you would do for a week in the

_ _ _ _ _ _ _ _ _ _

_____

_____

McGraw-Hill School Division

At Home: Have students write the words in the box on cards. Ask students to choose two cards and make up a sentence or riddle using the two words.

OUACHITA TECHNICAL COLLEGE

Vocabulary Review

Read the sentences. Circle the word that completes each sentence.
Use the pictures as clues.

1. We walk up the stairs to the _____.

   basement   attic

2. When Max was sick, he had many _____
   to keep him company.

   visitors   chairs

3. The sun came up at _____.

   dusk   dawn

Use each word below to write a sentence that tells about the picture.

4. **pattern**

   _____

5. **stumbled**

   _____

6. **palace**

   _____

At Home: Have students make up a fairy tale using the following words: **musician, imaginary, miserable, shallow, anxious, located, beauty, furniture, invented.** They can write and illustrate their story on paper folded in half to make a book to read to a younger child.

Book 3.1/Unit 3

111

McGraw-Hill School Division

Sequence of Events

Look at the pictures in the boxes. Decide what the sequence of events must be so that this story makes sense. In the empty boxes, draw two pictures that fit into the sequence of events. Then finish numbering the boxes in the order that makes most sense. Under each box, write a sentence that describes the action in that box.

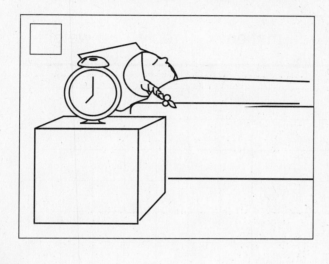

_____   _____

_____   _____

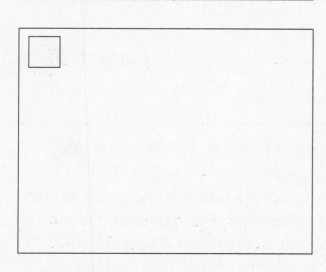

_____   _____

_____   _____

At Home: Use a comic strip such as those in the Sunday papers. Cut it apart into four or five sections. Ask students to put the comic back together in order.

112

Vocabulary

Use the grid below and the words in the box to make a crossword puzzle.
Print the words, using pencil, one letter to a box, connecting them as in a
crossword puzzle. Trace the puzzle to make a blank copy to trade with a
partner. Then number each word and write a clue. Solve each other's
puzzles.

completely	humans	meal	motion	reply	weight

Story Comprehension

Take a separate piece of paper and fold it in half. On the left-hand side,
make a list of the main characters from the story "The Terrible EEK." On
the right-hand side, across from each character's name, write down words
from the story that are important for that character. For example, across
from thief, you might write: human, roof, fell, and branch. Then cut your
paper in half down the middle. Exchange papers with a friend. See if your
friend can guess the characters that go with your words. See if you can do
the same for your friend's list.

At Home: Discuss a TV show together that features interesting characters.
Ask questions about the story, such as "Why did that character do that?" or
"What was the character feeling?" to explore the meaning in the story.

113–114

Book 3.2/Unit 1
The Terrible EEK

McGraw-Hill School Division

Use a Chart

Create a "My Friends" chart. Write titles at the top of each of the four columns for the different kinds of information such as **age** or **favorite food.** Ask several friends for information to fill in the chart. Give your chart to another friend and ask him or her questions about the friends on your chart, such as: Whose favorite food is pizza? See if they can answer the questions based on the information in your chart.

Names

_____ _____ _____ _____ _____

_____ _____ _____ _____ _____

_____ _____ _____ _____ _____

_____ _____ _____ _____ _____

_____ _____ _____ _____ _____

McGraw-Hill School Division

Book 3.2/Unit 1
The Terrible EEK

At Home: Make a chart of family members. Some suggested categories could be occupation, favorite hobby, favorite sport, and favorite movie.

115

Sequence of Events

Make up a funny story that has four steps in it. Include details to make it interesting. If possible, give your story a surprise ending. Draw the four steps out of order. Give your drawings to a partner. Have your partner write **1, 2, 3,** and **4** to show the correct order of events.

At Home: Take turns telling about a time when you were afraid of something. Ask children questions like "What happened before that?" and "What happened after?" to help them explain the sequence of events that took place.

Book 3.2/Unit 1
The Terrible EEK

Form Generalizations

Read the following paragraph. Then answer the questions below it.

    What is a friend? People have different answers. Some might say it's someone you like or someone who shares your interests. Others might say a friend is someone you can talk to and someone you trust. There are friends you see every day and some who may live far away. But no matter how you define it, one thing is definitely true. Friendship is one of the most important things in life.

1. What is the generalization in the story?

_____

_____

2. Do you agree with the generalization? Why? Why not?

_____

_____

3. Point out two examples of kinds of friends in the story.

_____

_____

4. What is your definition of a **friend?**

_____

_____

_____

_____

At Home: Ask students to choose one of the following topics: people who are angry, people who are scared or people who are curious. Ask them to form generalizations about people who feel these emotions.

McGraw-Hill School Division

Suffixes

| quick | soft | sad | dirt | fluff | sleep |

Attach a **y** or **ly** ending to the words in the box to make new words. Write your new words on the lines below. Then answer the questions below.

_____   _____

_____   _____

_____   _____

1. What is something you could do quickly? _____

_____

2. Who could speak softly? _____

3. When might you speak sadly? _____

_____

4. What is something that gets dirty a lot? _____

5. Name something that can be fluffy. _____

6. When might you be sleepy? _____

_____

7. Think of another word that ends in **ly.** Write a sentence using the

   word. Then circle the word. _____

_____

At Home: Ask students to look through a favorite book and find words that have **y** or **ly** endings. Then have students read the words to you and use a few of the words in new sentences.

118

Book 3.2/Unit 1
The Terrible EEK

McGraw-Hill School Division

Author's Purpose, Point of View

Read versions 1, 2, and 3 of the story "An Ant's Life." Answer the questions that follow the stories.

1. Billy watched the column of ants crawl over the bit of melting candy on the ground. He followed them to see where they went. Ants who had already visited the candy were disappearing into a hole in the dirt. Billy wondered what it was like down there.

2. "Mmmm, what's that over there? Smells good!" With his antennas, the ant sensed where the food was, and went to it. "Hey, stop pushing me from behind," he snarled at the ant behind him. "We've got to get this food back to the queen. We've got to work together." He hated these pushy ants who were always trying to be first.

3. Ants are social insects who live together in groups called colonies. Different ants do different kinds of work, but they all work for the common good of the group. There are thousands of different kinds of ants.

Which version tells the story from an ant's point of view? _____

Which version tells the story from the point of view of someone watching

some ants? _____

Which version tells the story from a scientific point of view, just giving us

facts about ants? _____

Draw a picture for each of the three versions of "An Ant's Life" on other paper. Label the pictures to show the point of view they illustrate.

At Home: Ask students to reread a favorite story. Talk with them about the point of view the story shows. How can they tell the point of view?

Vocabulary

| comforting | designed | dozens | encouraging | members | relatives |

On other paper, write a few paragraphs about a family gathering. Use as many vocabulary words from the box as you can. Be sure to include when and where this gathering takes place. Add a title to your story, and draw a picture to illustrate it. Trade stories with a partner. Does your partner have any ideas on improving the story?

Story Comprehension

The different parts of "In My Family" are almost like photographs in a family album.

You will need two sheets of paper. Draw five large boxes on the first sheet. In each box, draw or paste a picture of something that has happened in your life.

On the other sheet of paper, write a few sentences to describe what is happening in each picture. Cut out the pictures and the sentences. Arrange them in the order you like best. Make a family album like "In My Family."

At Home: Ask students to name their favorite photograph or drawing and explain why they like it.

120–121

Book 3.2/Unit 1
In My Family

McGraw-Hill School Division

Name_____ Date_____ **Extend** ◆122◆

Use a Diagram

Make a family tree for a made-up character. Put the made-up character on the bottom of the tree. Fill in the names of the parents and grandparents. On another piece of paper, write something interesting about a member of this family.

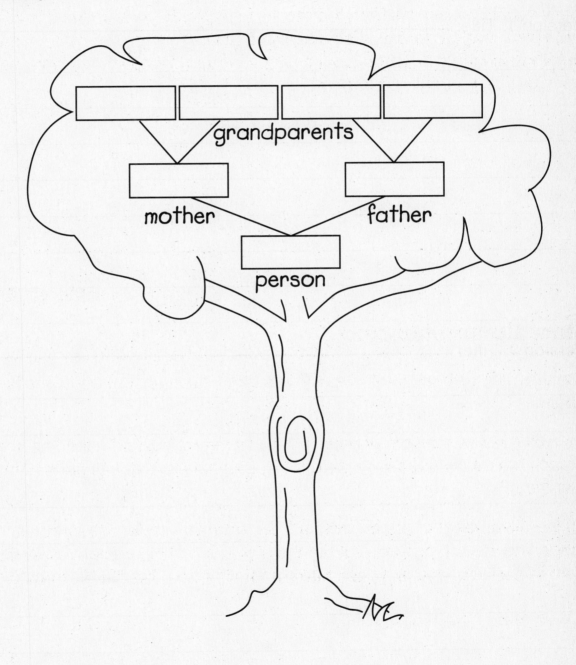

grandparents

mother   father

person

McGraw-Hill School Division

Book 3.2/Unit 1
In My Family

At Home: Look together for diagrams in newspapers and magazines. Discuss how information is organized in each diagram.

122

Author's Purpose, Point of View

Think of an exciting event, such as a school play or a spelling bee. Then write about it in two different ways. Write one version from your point of view. Write a second version from the point of view of a friend or family member at the event. Give a title to each version.

Version 1. Title: _____

_____

_____

_____

_____

_____

_____

_____

Version 2. Title: _____

_____

_____

_____

_____

_____

_____

_____

At Home: Ask students to discuss something that happened in school from their own point of view. Then ask them to think about and explain how the same situation might appear from a classmate's point of view.

123

Book 3.2/Unit 1
In My Family

McGraw-Hill School Division

Sequence of Events

Read the two events in the boxes. Think of events that could fit before and after them. Write the events in the boxes. Then read your story to a friend.

1.

2.

Then it began to rain.

Lightning flashed.

3.

4.

5.

Jake woke up and looked out

the window.

6.

Book 3.2/Unit 1
In My Family

At Home: Ask students to list four events of their day in the order they happened.

124

McGraw-Hill School Division

Figurative Language

Read the poem about winter. Answer the questions that follow.

Winter

Winter feels like a soft, warm cocoon that you're wrapped inside of.
Winter looks like a picture postcard with mountains and snow.
Winter tastes like an icicle, hard and cold on your tongue.
Winter smells like caramel popcorn, sweet and hot.
Winter sounds like children's voices ringing out in the cold.

1. Name the five senses used in this poem.

   _____ _____ _____

   _____ _____

2. Which comparison in the poem do you like the best? _____

   _____

   Why? _____

3. Make up your own comparison for winter. _____

Choose one of the four seasons and write your own poem about it. Make comparisons that use the five senses (tastes like, sounds like, smells like, feels like, looks like). Give your poem a title.

Title: _____

_____

_____

_____

_____

_____

At Home: Ask students to think of some things that are found at home, such as refrigerator, sofa, and television. For each object, make a comparison to something, using one of the five senses.

125

Book 3.2/Unit 1
In My Family

McGraw-Hill School Division

Cause and Effect

Read the cause or the effect in each pair. Write a possible missing cause or effect.

Cause	**Effect**
Suddenly, all the lights went out at the birthday party.	
Matt held out an apple to the pony.	
	Some milk spilled on the floor.

Keep a Cause-Effect Journal. Staple together several pieces of paper. On each left hand page write: **Causes.** On each right hand page, write: **Effects.** Every day make an entry in this journal.

At Home: Talk with students about things that happened this week. Ask the student to tell which events caused things to happen.

McGraw-Hill School Division

Vocabulary

discovered	insects	remains	ribs	tough	treat

Imagine you are a scientist studying wildlife in the desert. On other paper, write a journal entry, using as many vocabulary words from the box as you can. Exchange your journal entry with a partner. Find the vocabulary words. Was each word used correctly? Tell your partner how to fix any mistakes.

Extend ◈ 128

Story Comprehension

The cactus in the story grows and changes over 200 years. Think of something else that grows or changes over a period of time, such as a tree, or your town. Draw a long time line to show a time period. Then make drawings or get pictures to show how the thing or place has changed, and attach them to the time line.

At Home: Ask students to think of how a person grows and matures over a long period of time. If possible, use pictures in a magazine to discuss how people grow and change.

127–128

Book 3.2/Unit 1
Cactus Hotel

McGraw-Hill School Division

Use a Chart

Fill in the chart with as many kinds of changes and growth as you can think of for each of the categories.

Changes and Growth

Seasons	Fall	Winter	Spring	Summer
Trees/Plants				
Animals				
You				

Use another sheet of paper. Draw a picture for each season of the year based on the information in your chart. Each picture should include a tree or plant, animal, and you. Label each picture with the name of the season that it shows.

McGraw-Hill School Division

Book 3.2/Unit 1
Cactus Hotel

At Home: Ask students to think about their own development from birth to the present. Encourage them to make charts, decide what the column headings should be, and fill them in.

Cause and Effect

Think of an activity you would like to plan. Make up a sequence of things that relate to that plan and then affect another chain of events. For example, plan a birthday party that has different ways of affecting parents, friends and their families, your family, and the activity itself.

Cause   Effect

[blank chart with four pairs of boxes connected by arrows]

At Home: Ask students to choose one of the following topics and talk about causes and effects for that topic. Suggested topics: a sporting event; a major snowstorm or weather event; or an argument between friends.

Book 3.2/Unit 1
Cactus Hotel

McGraw-Hill School Division

Sequence of Events

Tigers play Lions today

Imagine you are a radio announcer for one of the following events: a sports event; a school event or celebration; or a birthday party. On other paper, write down what you would say as you report on the sequence of events that takes place. Try to describe the sequence of events in a way that makes it as exciting as possible for your listeners.

Now, find an object that you could use as a pretend microphone. Use it to read your description of the event. Try to read in a way that makes the event exciting. Afterwards, ask your listeners questions about the event, such as: What happened at the beginning? What happened at the end? What was the most exciting part of the event?

At Home: Ask students to tell the sequence of events in preparing a meal. Talk about how a recipe is a sequence of events.

Suffixes

Make new words by adding the suffixes **y, ly,** and **able** to the following words. Check the spellings of the new words in a dictionary.

friend _____

love _____

thorn _____

adore _____

gentle _____

angry _____

What happens when you add the **able** ending to the words **love** and **adore?**

_____

What happens when you add the **ly** ending to the word **gentle?**

_____

What happens when you add the **ly** ending to the word **angry?**

_____

On a separate piece of paper, write a paragraph using as many of the above words as possible.

At Home: Ask students to make a list of words that end in **y, ly,** and **able.** Read them aloud. Ask students to see what happens when the ending is removed from each word. Ask what other word is left.

132

Book 3.2/Unit 1
Cactus Hotel

McGraw-Hill School Division

Form Generalizations

Think of two things that could be examples of each generalization. Draw pictures of your examples in the boxes below the generalizations. Label your examples.

Mammals are animals that have fur.

Most plants have leaves.

Eating a good breakfast helps you start the day off right.

On other paper, write a paragraph about one of the generalizations. Use one of the sentences above as an opening sentence. Then include examples that illustrate the generalization. You can use the examples you have already drawn pictures of.

At Home: Tell students "The library has many different kinds of books." Ask students to give you examples that illustrate this generalization. Ask questions such as: What are your favorite kinds of books?

Vocabulary

adult	calm	feast	mammal	swallow	vast

On another piece of paper, write a paragraph. Use as many of the words in the vocabulary box above as you can. Then erase those vocabulary words or cover them with tape. Give your paragraph to a partner. Take your partner's paragraph. Fill in the blanks.

Extend ◀135▶

Story Comprehension

Use an encyclopedia or another book to find more information about whales. Write five interesting things you learned from your research, about blue whales or about other kinds of whales.

_____

_____

_____

_____

_____

_____

_____

_____

McGraw-Hill School Division

At Home: Ask students to explain what an index is and how to use an index in a science book to find answers.

134–135

Book 3.2/Unit 1
Big Blue Whale

Use a Graph

Read the paragraph. Then fill in the bar graph to show the lengths of each animal. Then answer the question below.

   Blue whales can grow to be 100 feet long. Full-grown anaconda snakes can grow as long as 33 feet. Most men are around 6 feet tall. Crocodiles can be up to 20 feet long. A great white shark can also be up to 20 feet long.

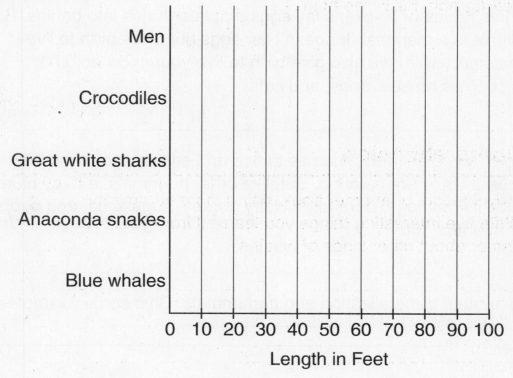

Length in Feet

What does the chart tell you about the lengths of the different animals?

_____

_____

_____

_____

At Home: Ask students to find the height of five different people in their family or of friends. Ask them to create a bar graph showing the height of each person.

Form Generalizations

Write generalizations about mammals from the following information:

The blue whale is a mammal. That's why, even though it lives in the water, it needs to come up for air in order to breathe. Seals and dolphins are also mammals. They also need to come up to breathe air.

_____

Birds such as robins or chickens lay eggs that later hatch into babies. But the blue whale is a mammal. It doesn't lay eggs but gives birth to live young. Seals and walruses also give birth to live young. So do other mammals such as horses, dogs, and cats.

_____

The young of some animals, such as turtles and snakes, go off on their own as soon as they are hatched. But, like other mammals, a baby blue whale needs its mother to care for it. Baby horses, dogs, cats, and people need their mothers, too.

_____

Now write another generalization about mammals. Give some examples.

Generalization: _____

_____

_____

_____

_____

_____

_____

At Home: Ask students to listen to these generalizations and talk about whether or not they are true. **All dogs bark too much. All cats are finicky.**

137

Book 3.2/Unit 1
Big Blue Whale

McGraw-Hill School Division

Author's Purpose, Point of View

Think about some books you have read. Write examples of books written for different purposes suggested below.

Purpose: to inform

Example: _____

Purpose: to entertain

Example: _____

Purpose: to make us think

Example: _____

On a separate piece of paper, write the name of a book in your class or school library. Exchange papers with a friend. Write the purpose of the book you each have written. (If necessary, examine the book.) Then check each other's answers. Do you agree?

At Home: Ask students to choose a favorite book and reread the opening paragraphs. Discuss what the author's purpose was in the opening paragraphs.

Figurative Language

Write down a few examples of figurative language used to describe the whale in "Big Blue Whale."

_____

_____

_____

_____

_____

Think of a pet or another animal you like. Write three comparisons using figurative language to describe what the animal looks like. Make your comparisons as exact as you can.

_____

_____

_____

_____

_____

_____

At Home: Ask students to describe someone they know using figurative language.

Book 3.2/Unit 1
Big Blue Whale

139

McGraw-Hill School Division

Cause and Effect

Write down as many different causes and effects as you can think of for the following event.

School was closed on Friday.

Causes:

_____

_____

_____

_____

Effects:

_____

_____

_____

_____

On other paper, choose another event and write a paragraph in which you explain the causes of the event, and the effects. Decide whether you're going to write first about the causes or the effects.

At Home: Let students ask you about your day. Encourage them to ask questions such as, "What caused that to happen?" or "What was the effect of that?" Have students write down the results of their cause-effect interviews.

Vocabulary

clams	compared	experts	gain	powdered	switch

Fit the words from the box into a crossword puzzle. Each word must share a letter with another word. Number each word. Write **Across** and **Down** clues for each word on other paper.

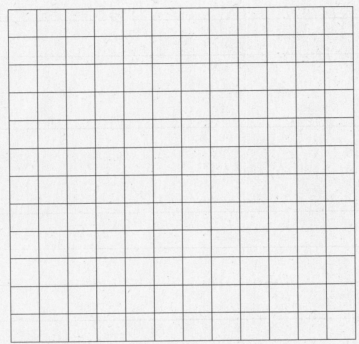

Story Comprehension

On a separate piece of paper, write a news report on the story of "J.J.'s Big Day." Be sure to answer the following questions: **What** happened? **Where** and **when** did it happen? **How** did it happen? **Why** did it happen? **Who** was involved? **What** were the results?

At Home: Ask students to write a news report about something that happened in the classroom. Have them answer the questions: What? Where? When? Who? How? Why?

141–142

Book 3.2/Unit 1
J.J.'s Big Day

McGraw-Hill School Division

Use a Graph

Do research. Ask everyone in your class what their favorite color is. Tally the answers on the sheet below. Then enter the results of the research on the bar graph below.

Tally Sheet

Red _____

Green _____

Yellow _____

Blue _____

Orange _____

Pink _____

Other _____

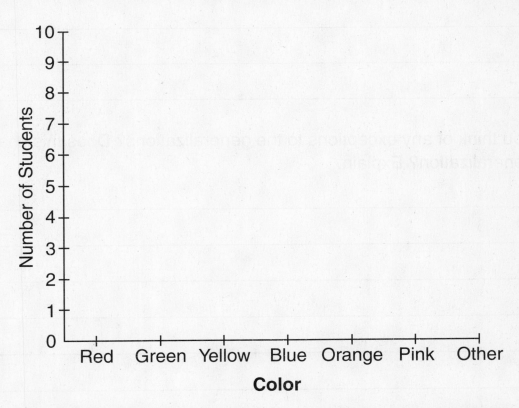

Book 3.2/Unit 1
J.J.'s Big Day

At Home: Ask students about the results of their polls. Discuss different ways polling and then graphing the information can be useful.

143

Form Generalizations

Read the generalizations. Then provide two or three examples that support the generalization.

1. Many people like to eat pizza.

_____

_____

_____

2. Dogs are popular as pets.

_____

_____

_____

3. Many people wear sneakers.

_____

_____

_____

Did you think of any exceptions to the generalizations? Does this change the generalization? Explain.

_____

_____

_____

_____

_____

At Home: Make a generalization about your family. Have students give an example that supports the generalization.

Book 3.2/Unit 1
J.J.'s Big Day

144

McGraw-Hill School Division

Figurative Language

Complete the comparisons in the following paragraph by filling in the blanks.

The animals filed into a cave as big as _____. Then a terrible storm came up. It thundered like _____, and the lightning flashed brighter than _____. The rain poured down like _____. The animals were as frightened as _____. But the wise old owl told them, "Don't worry, soon the sun will come out and shine brighter than _____." Sure enough, the owl was right. Very soon it stopped raining, the sun came out, and a beautiful rainbow arched in the sky like a _____.

Look out the window for a few minutes and take notes on what you see.

Window Notes

_____

_____

_____

_____

_____

On a separate piece of paper, write a paragraph about what you saw, using several examples of figurative language.

At Home: Ask students to look through magazines or books for examples of figurative language. Talk about the effect of the figurative language. Does it make the writing funnier, more interesting, or more imaginative?

Suffixes

| stick | ice | velvet | sudden | quiet | stubborn | comfort | reach |

See how many new words you can make out of the words in the box above by adding the suffixes **y, ly,** or **able.** Remember that for words that end in *e,* you have to drop the **e** before adding the suffix.

_____   _____

_____   _____

_____   _____

_____   _____

_____   _____

_____   _____

_____   _____

On a separate piece of paper, write a story using as many of the above words with suffixes as you can. When you finish, tape pieces of paper over the words with suffixes. Then exchange papers with a friend. Ask your friend to figure out what words go in the empty spaces. See if you can figure out the correct words that go in your friend's story.

At Home: Help students make a list of words with the **y, ly,** or **able** endings from a newspaper or magazine article. Ask students to read the words to you and explain what the suffix endings are.

146

Book 3.2/Unit 1
J.J.'s Big Day

Vocabulary Review

hear	soft	fish	excited	height	clams

Read each sentence. If it makes sense, put a check. If it does not, circle the word that doesn't fit and replace it with a word from the box.

☐ **1.** The clay was so hard that it was easy to work with.

_____

☐ **2.** His ribs are bones found in his chest.

_____

☐ **3.** My relatives came to visit on the holiday.

_____

☐ **4.** Humans live in the sea all the time.

_____

☐ **5.** The dog discovered the bone in the yard.

_____

☐ **6.** I use my ears to swallow.

_____

☐ **7.** He was so calm that he jumped up and down.

_____

☐ **8.** The dogs have two shells to protect them.

_____

☐ **9.** His weight was 5 feet 7 inches tall.

_____

☐ **10.** The big feast made me so full.

_____

At Home: Ask students to write the words **relatives, weight, ribs, feast,** and **clams** on cards. Take turns choosing a card and making up three sentences to go with the word. Set a timer for one minute as a challenge.

Vocabulary Review

Cut out the word cards, or copy the words onto index cards.

Play with a friend.

Pick a card. Use the word on the card in a sentence to begin a story.

Ask your friend to pick a card and use the word on the card in a sentence to continue your story. Take turns picking cards and telling the story.

insects	humans	feast
swallows	adult	completely
meal	motion	reply
discovered	treat	comforting
designed	dozens	encouraging
members	vast	compared
experts	gain	powdered
switched	swallow	tough

McGraw-Hill School Division

At Home: Encourage students to put the word cards in alphabetical order.

Book 3.2/Unit 1

Judgments and Decisions

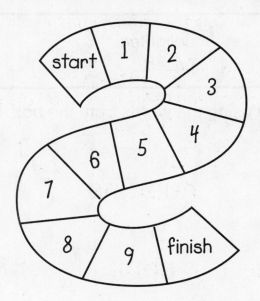

Play Smart!

Throw a die and move a marker along the game board. Find the statement below that matches the number. If the statement is a good decision, roll again. If it isn't, go back and start again. Think about what makes a good decision.

1. Wear a sweater when it's cold outside.

2. Never eat your food.

3. Wear seat belts when riding in a car.

4. Put your shoes on before your pants.

5. Learn from people who know more than you.

6. Forget to brush your teeth.

7. Look before crossing the street.

8. Don't write thank-you letters.

9. Never go to sleep.

Book 3.2/Unit 2
Lon Po Po

At Home: Have students think of several animals and write why some are safe to pet and some aren't.

149

Vocabulary

claws	delighted	disguised
furious	paced	route

Make up a fable or story using the words from the box. Choose one of the words and use it twice.

Story Comprehension

The setting of a story, where it takes place, can be very important. The story of Lon Po Po is set in China. Write a paragraph about how the story would be different if it were set where you live.

_____

_____

_____

_____

_____

_____

_____

At Home: Have students find a newspaper article about another country and write a sentence describing the article.

150–151

Book 3.2/Unit 2
Lon Po Po

Read a Newspaper

Some stories in newspapers have pictures. The pictures give an impression of what the story is about. Photographs in newspapers and magazines usually have captions. Captions are words that describe the picture. Write captions for each of the pictures below.

_____   _____

_____   _____

_____   _____

_____   _____

McGraw-Hill School Division

Book 3.2/Unit 2
Lon Po Po

At Home: Ask students to choose an article in the newspaper and draw the photo that might go along with it.

Judgments and Decisions

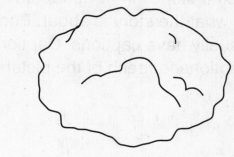
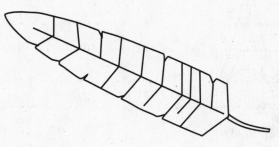

Write two sentences about each of the objects above. In the first sentence, describe an activity you **would** do with the object. In the second sentence, write something you **wouldn't do** with the object. Then write the reasons you had for deciding what you did.

_____

_____

_____

_____

_____

_____

_____

_____

_____

_____

At Home: Imagine being 100 years old. Write a paragraph describing what if would feel like to be 100 and what the world around you would be like.

Book 3.2/Unit 2
Lon Po Po

Summarize

_____   _____   _____
_____   _____   _____
_____   _____   _____

_____   _____   _____
_____   _____   _____
_____   _____   _____

A **summary** tells the most important parts of a story and leaves out many of the details. Use the time line above to summarize your day yesterday. Write the six most important events that happened to you. The events could include ordinary things like going to school, as well as anything special or exciting. If something important happened in your family or in the news, you can include that, too. Tell why you chose the events you did.

_____

_____

_____

_____

_____

_____

_____

_____

At Home: Have students write a summary of a favorite story. Help them differentiate between important events that should be included and details that can be left out.

Context Clues

A story is like a path that leads to the place the story ends. Use the imaginary road. Draw pictures and describe what happens in Lon Po Po. Be sure to include important details and context clues. Show your "story map" to someone who hasn't read "Lon Po Po."

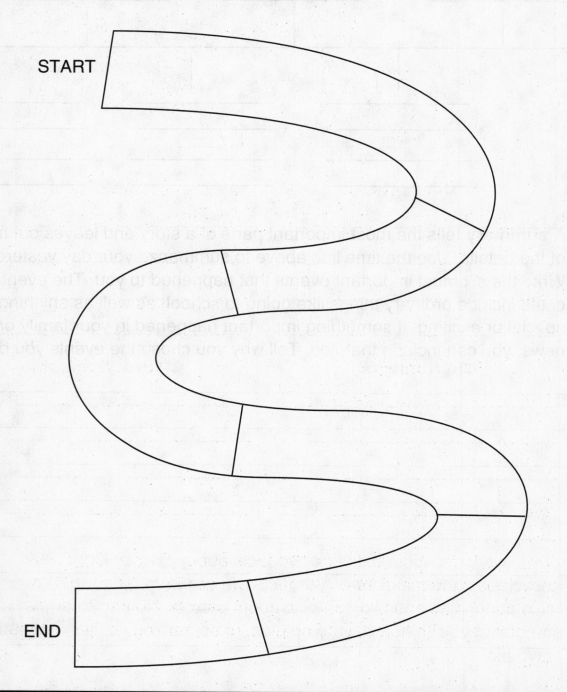

START

END

At Home: Have students look in newspapers and magazines and cut out the articles they find interesting. Then help them use context clues to identify the meanings of difficult words.

155

Book 3.2/Unit 2
Lon Po Po

McGraw-Hill School Division

Fact and Nonfact

Cat Facts   **Parrot Facts**

_____   _____
_____   _____
_____   _____
_____   _____

Cat Nonfacts   **Parrot Nonfacts**

_____   _____
_____   _____
_____   _____
_____   _____

Write two facts about cats and two facts about parrots. Check the encyclopedia to make sure your facts are accurate. Then write two non-facts about cats and two nonfacts about parrots. Nonfacts can be something you've heard, your opinion, or something you've just made up. Have fun!

At Home: Have students cut out a newspaper article about an animal and write a fact they have learned from the article.

Vocabulary

dog	goat	turtle	porcupine	ostrich	cricket
attack	bother	expects	label	rapidly	temperature

Pair an animal from the top row with a word from the bottom row, and write a sentence using each pair.

_____

_____

_____

_____

_____

_____

_____

_____

_____

Story Comprehension

Play Pin the Quill on the Porcupine. Make five porcupine quills from construction paper. On each one, write a porcupine fact or fable. Compare your porcupine facts and fables with your classmates' to see how many different ones the class wrote. Then take turns pinning your quills on a large, quill-less paper porcupine in the classroom.

At Home: Show students photographs of armor, cars, buildings, and clothing. Have them write which one is the most like a turtle shell and how they made their choice.

157–158

Book 3.2/Unit 2
Animal Fact/Animal Fable

McGraw-Hill School Division

Read a Newspaper

Choose an article from the front page of a newspaper. See how many facts you can find in your article, and write them below. Then choose an article from the sports page of a newspaper. Write the facts you find in that article. Compare the two articles. Which has more facts? Why?

Front Page Facts _____
_____
_____
_____
_____
_____

Sports Facts _____
_____
_____
_____
_____
_____

Compare Articles _____
_____
_____
_____
_____

McGraw-Hill School Division

Book 3.2/Unit 2
Animal Fact/Animal Fable

At Home: Have students draw a picture of their feet. Have them write a fun fact about their feet, then a fun fable.

Fact and Nonfact

Read each sentence below. In the first blank, write whether the sentence is a fact or a fable. Then, if the sentence is a fact, write a fable about the same animal. If the sentence is a fable, write a fact about the same animal.

Goats sometimes eat metal cans. _____

_____

Dogs wag their tails. _____

_____

Ostriches hide their heads in the sand. _____

_____

Turtles do not walk out of their shells. _____

_____

Porcupines defend themselves with their quills. _____

_____

At Home: Have students invent fables about other animals—things people might believe, but are not really true.

160

Book 3.2/Unit 2
Animal Fact/Animal Fable

McGraw-Hill School Division

Summarize

Pretend you are going on vacation for two weeks, and your friend is going to care for your pet while you are away. Think of all the things you do to care for your pet. Then think of just the most important parts of your pet's care. Use these to write a summary of what your friend needs to do while you are away. Choose an imaginary pet if you do not have a real one.

_____

_____

_____

_____

_____

_____

At Home: Have students summarize a movie they saw recently or an episode of a favorite television show. Discuss which events are important to the summary and which events can be left out.

Context Clues

The chirps of a cricket change with the temperature. Which of the items below change with the temperature? Write how it changes.

tea kettle _____

_____

_____

candle _____

_____

_____

thermometer _____

_____

_____

radio _____

_____

_____

At Home: Have students choose their favorite animal from the selection and tell why it is their favorite.

162

Book 3.2/Unit 2
Animal Fact/Animal Fable

McGraw-Hill School Division

Main Idea

What if you were the news director of your local television station? Think of five news stories from your home, your town, or your school. Make a list. Then order the stories from most important to least important. For each story, decide the main idea that you want people to understand. Write your five main ideas below. Ask other students to help and then present your very own news report.

_____

_____

_____

_____

_____

At Home: Have students listen to the headline story on the radio or television news. Then suggest they write a few sentences telling the main idea of that story.

Vocabulary

advice	curious	discuss
experiment	hero	scientific

Write a paragraph about a famous hero. Use as many words from the box as you can. Then erase those words or cover them with tape. Exchange paragraphs with a partner and fill in the blanks.

Story Comprehension

Benjamin Franklin created many useful inventions, including the lightning rod, the Franklin stove for heating homes, and bifocal glasses. Think of an invention that would make your life easier. One example might be a personal helicopter that would fly you from your front door to the front door of your school every day. Describe your invention and tell something about how you would make it. Draw a picture of your invention.

At Home: Have students discuss their inventions, using as many vocabulary words as they can.

164-165

Book 3.2/Unit 2
The Many Lives of Benjamin Franklin

McGraw-Hill School Division

Name_____ Date_____ **Extend** ◇166

Follow Directions

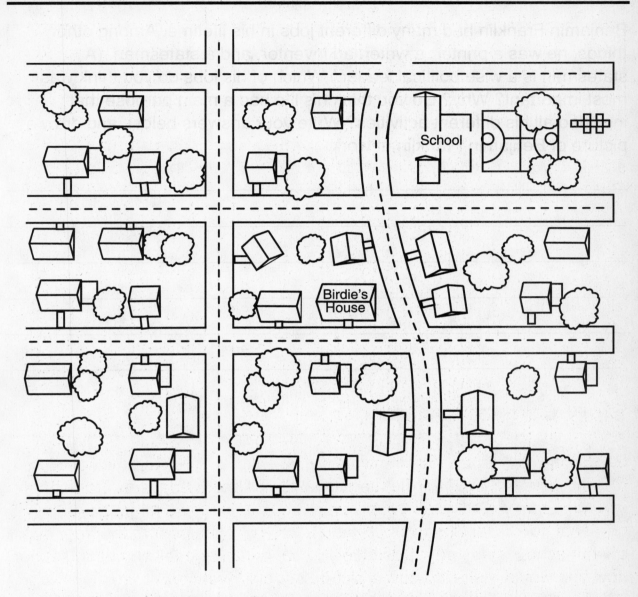

It is Birdie's first day at school, and she doesn't know how to get there. Look at the map above and write clear directions for Birdie to go from her house to school. Be sure to label landmarks on the map that she might recognize along the way.

McGraw-Hill School Division

Book 3.2/Unit 2
**The Many Lives of
Benjamin Franklin**

At Home: Have students draw a map of the route they take to school.

166

Main Idea

Benjamin Franklin had many different jobs in his lifetime. Among other things, he was a printer, a writer, an inventor, and a statesman. (A statesman is a wise political leader.) Which of his jobs do you think was most important? Why? Do you think his life had a main purpose that included all his different activities? Write your answers below, and draw a picture of Benjamin Franklin at work.

_____

_____

_____

_____

_____

_____

McGraw-Hill School Division

At Home: Have students think of their favorite song. Ask them to write the main idea of the words. If the song does not have words, ask them to write what the music is trying to express.

Book 3.2/Unit 2
**The Many Lives of
Benjamin Franklin**

Judgments and Decisions

Read the five-day weather forecast and the list of activities below. Choose an activity or two that would be good for each day, based on the weather forecast. Write a sentence telling why those activities would be appropriate for the weather.

Monday	Tuesday	Wednesday	Thursday	Friday

go to the beach
go to the zoo
visit a museum
go skiing
look up at the clouds
take an umbrella
wear a hat and scarf
play soccer

Monday _____

Tuesday _____

Wednesday _____

Thursday _____

Friday _____

At Home: Have students write down how they predict the weather or find out about weather predictions.

McGraw-Hill School Division

Root Words

Words that measure units of time are often root words. Add *bi* to the beginning of *weekly,* and you have *biweekly,* something that happens twice a week.

Add *bi* to other words that also measure time. See how many other words you can make! (Hint to get you started: *bi* + *cycle* = *bicycle*)

_____

_____

_____

_____

At Home: Have students make sentences from the words they listed.

169

Book 3.2/Unit 2
**The Many Lives of
Benjamin Franklin**

McGraw-Hill School Division

Summarize

To summarize is to make a long story short. One way to do that is to include only the important points or events. Imagine what you did yesterday. Draw a picture of yourself doing it. Describe the picture and tell why you chose what you did.

_____

_____

_____

_____

At Home: Have students ask someone to describe his or her day. Have students write a short summary of the most important parts of the story.

Vocabulary

avoid	brief	frequently
gradual	periods	report

Which words from the box above complete the sentence below?

_____ the weather _____ mentions

_____ showers or _____ of

_____ clearing.

Story Comprehension

Make up a menu using the various foods that fall from the sky in the town of Chewandswallow. Draw your menu so that it looks like a menu from a real restaurant.

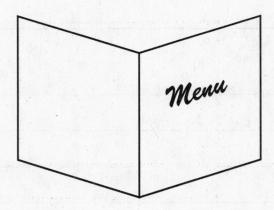

At Home: Have students cut out pictures of food from advertisements. On a piece of paper have them draw a picture of themselves standing on the ground. Then they can tape on the pictures as if the food were coming from the sky.

Book 3.2/Unit 2
Cloudy With a Chance of Meatballs

McGraw-Hill School Division

Read Signs

Thousands of tiny green frogs once rained down on a town in Greece. Scientists think that a whirlwind sucked up the frogs from North African marshes. A fast air stream then carried them 500 miles to Greece. Many frogs survived and lived happily in their new home.

Think of another unusual weather sign that could warn people about the dangers of strange weather. Write the kind of weird weather on the lines and draw your sign in the box.

For example:

```
┌─────────────────┐
│                 │
│  WATCH OUT      │
│                 │
│  FOR FALLING    │
│                 │
│  GREEN PEAS     │
│                 │
└─────────────────┘
_____
```

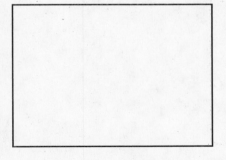

Book 3.2/Unit 2
**Cloudy With a Chance
of Meatballs**

At Home: Have students create a sign to go on the door of their room. Ask them to explain the sign they make.

173

McGraw-Hill School Division

Summarize

An autobiography is a book in which a person writes his or her own life story. Choose some important events in your life so far. Then write three sentences that summarize your autobiography, or life story. Draw a picture to illustrate one of your sentences.

_____

_____

_____

_____

_____

At Home: Have students think of their favorite bedtime story. Have them write a one-sentence summary.

174

Book 3.2/Unit 2
Cloudy With a Chance of Meatballs

Main Idea

> 2 eggs
> 1 celery stalk chopped
> a pinch of salt
> a pinch of pepper
> 5 drops of olive oil

Think of a few of your favorite foods. There are probably different spices used in making the food, but the main ingredient gives food its taste. Create a recipe, but instead of using food, use some things that you do on an ordinary day. You might have a cup of school, a teaspoon of television, a pinch of soccer. Write down your recipe. Then write a paragraph describing what your recipe will make. State the main idea of your paragraph.

_____

_____

_____

_____

_____

_____

_____

_____

McGraw-Hill School Division

At Home: Tell students to look around a room in their house. Ask them to choose the most important parts of the room and tell why.

Vocabulary

energy	entire	future
model	pollution	produce

Write each vocabulary word on a different card. Write the definitions on other cards. Play a matching game with a partner. Place the cards face down. Turn over two cards. If the word matches the definition, keep the cards. If the cards don't match, turn them over and let your partner have a turn.

Story Comprehension

Scientists help us use the power of the sun and wind in our lives. Pretend you are a scientist. Think of another source of power, and tell how it could be turned into energy. On another sheet of paper, draw a picture of your new source of energy. Describe what it is and how it works.

_____

_____

_____

_____

_____

_____

At Home: Have students count the things in their house that use energy. What uses the most? What uses the least?

178–179

Book 3.2/Unit 2
Pure Power!

McGraw-Hill School Division

Read an Ad

Advertisements try to get us to buy things. Look at advertisements in newspapers and magazines. Then make your own advertisement to sell windmills. Draw a picture of your product. Make sure you explain how windmills are helpful and why people would want one or more!

_____

_____

_____

_____

_____

_____

_____

_____

At Home: Look at ads in magazines and newspapers or on television. Talk about what you see. Are the products really necessary? Are they as good as the ads make them sound?

McGraw-Hill School Division

Fact and Nonfact

Check out your knowledge of power! Below are some statements about energy and its uses. Some are facts and some are nonfacts. Write TRUE next to the facts, and FALSE next to the nonfacts.

_____ Fossil fuels are formed from plants and animals.

_____ Solar energy uses power from the wind.

_____ The human body uses food as its fuel.

_____ Power plants burn fossil fuels to make energy.

_____ Windmill farms grow apples and pears in long rows.

_____ Solar energy is cleaner than energy from burning coal.

Write four more of your own facts and nonfacts about energy.

_____

_____

_____

_____

At Home: Discuss with students how their bodies run on energy and where that energy comes from.

181

Book 3.2/Unit 2
Pure Power!

McGraw-Hill School Division

Root Words

Many words in the English language come from roots in the ancient language of Latin. Several root words about energy and its uses began many years ago as Latin words. For example, *automobile* is made from two Latin words—*auto,* which means *self,* and *mobilis,* meaning *moving.*

Look at these Latin root words. See if you can think of energy-related English words we use today that came from these roots.

Latin Root	**English Word**
sol (means sun)	_____
pollutus (to make dirty)	_____
oleum (means oil)	_____

Use each of the English words in a sentence.

_____

_____

_____

McGraw-Hill School Division

At Home: Together with the students, look up some other energy-related words in the dictionary to discover their roots.

Context Clues

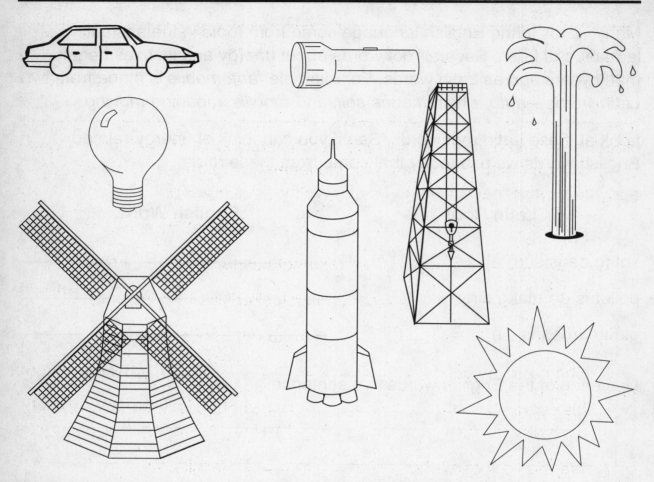

Which pictures above show sources of energy? Draw circles around those pictures. Which pictures show objects that use energy? Draw squares around those pictures.

Write a short paragraph about how you use energy. Also talk about ways you can save energy. Why is saving energy important?

_____

_____

_____

_____

At Home: Invite students to make their own windmills. Cut out cardboard triangles. Twist them so that they catch the wind. Use a pin and place three triangles on the end of a pencil. Have students write about why their windmills do or do not work.

183

Book 3.2/Unit 2
Pure Power!

McGraw-Hill School Division

Vocabulary Review

future	delighted	pollution	label
model	reports	advice	curious
hero	avoid	route	

Read these sentences, and use the words above to fill in the blanks. Use one blank for each letter. Watch for the letters in the boxes. They will spell a mystery word that will help you answer the final question!

1. I was — — — — — — [t] — — that we won.

2. The — — — — [e] we take gets us to town the fastest.

3. The [m] — — — — car almost looked like the real one.

4. I write — — [p] — — — — about books I read.

5. She gave me good — — — — — [e] to try my best in school.

6. Max was — — [r] — — — — about how the magician did his tricks.

7. We are very careful to [a] — — — — accidents.

8. The — — [t] — — — will bring many new and exciting things.

9. A way to try and stop — — — — [u] — — — — is to recycle.

10. He was my — — [r] — because he was brave, smart, and kind.

11. We read the — — — [e] — to see what is in the food.

Mystery Question: What is the _____ today?

_____

At Home: Use the same vocabulary words to create a new puzzle with a different "mystery word."

Vocabulary Review

Write a paragraph about making something using as many as the vocabulary words below as you can. Make a second copy of your paragraph with blanks where the vocabulary words should be. Exchange paragraphs with a partner and see if he or she can fill in the blanks.

disguised	experiment	frequently	gradual
curious	discuss	produce	
energy	entire	rapidly	expects

_____

_____

_____

_____

_____

_____

_____

_____

_____

_____

_____

_____

_____

_____

At Home: Ask students to write their own definitions of the vocabulary words above. Discuss their answers.

McGraw-Hill School Division

Make Inferences

Sometimes we are only told part of a story. Often we only see part of an activity. Read the phrases below. Uncover one phrase at a time. Try to figure out what activity is being described. See how many clues it takes to come to your conclusion.

1. A person is holding an object.

2. The object is made of wood.

3. The person is using two hands to perform this activity.

4. Other people listen while the person performs this activity.

5. The object has strings.

6. The person is part of an orchestra.

7. The name of the object begins with a "v" and ends with an "n."

Think of your own activity. On a separate piece of paper make a list of clues. Share your list with other students and see if they can guess.

At Home: Have students draw a picture of an activity. Ask them to cut the drawing into parts and use the parts as pieces of a homemade puzzle.

Vocabulary

| accept | equipment | invisible | mistakes | perform | talented |

Write each word in the box on a card. Write definitions for each word on other cards. Play a matching game with a partner. Place the cards face down. Turn over two cards at a time. If the word matches the definition, keep the cards. If not, turn them over and let your partner have a turn.

Story Comprehension

"The Bat Boy and His Violin" is fun to read aloud. Get together with students in a group. Find sections of the story where people are speaking to each other. Write out the dialogue. Then select parts to play and act out the story. Rehearse the selection and then perform it for another class.

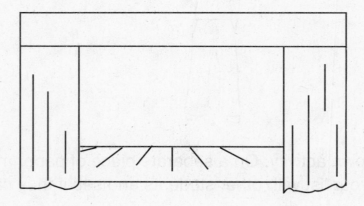

At Home: Ask students to make up their own dialogue for a short conversation. Invite them to use realistic dialogue so that their characters seem like real people.

McGraw-Hill School Division

Use the Library

A library is a place for exploring. Discovering something new is like following a path. One book leads to another book. Go to your library. Pick a book that you already know about. Who is the author? What is the subject? Find another book written by the same author or about the same subject. Do the same for the second book. Be an explorer by following the trail of the books. Write in the names of the books you found on the trail below.

Book 3.2/Unit 3
The Bat Boy and His Violin

At Home: Have students write about their favorite book and why they like it.

189

Make Inferences

In most stories characters show their feelings by what they say or do. In the story "The Bat Boy and His Violin," think about how Reginald's father feels about the violin. Does he change his mind? Below are some quotations from the story. Try to infer from the quotations how Reginald's father feels toward the violin.

"Is—Reginald—at—it—again?" _____

_____

"It's a wonder that boy don't sprout mushrooms." _____

_____

"This might inspire you to become a ball player the way your ol' man was."

_____

"Good thing we got us a gifted little bat boy." _____

_____

"We prefer to call it a *violin*." _____

_____

Think of something that you feel strongly about. Write your own quotations and then share them with a partner. Can your partner guess what you were feeling?

At Home: Have students look in the story and find clues that reveal how the baseball players feel toward Reginald's violin.

190

Book 3.2/Unit 3
The Bat Boy and His Violin

McGraw-Hill School Division

Author's Purpose, Point of View

There are many kinds of writing. Writing can persuade, inform, and entertain. Write a few sentences about the cans of soup pictured below. Beneath the first can of soup, try to persuade us to buy the soup. Beneath the second can, give some information about the soup. Beneath the third can, tell a joke or funny story about the soup.

_____   _____

_____   _____

_____   _____

_____   _____

_____

_____

_____

_____

At Home: Have students find a newspaper article and decide what the author's purpose is. Ask them to write out their reasons.

Multiple-Meaning Words

The following words have more than one meaning. In the boxes provided draw two pictures that describe two meanings of the word. The first one is done for you.

deck

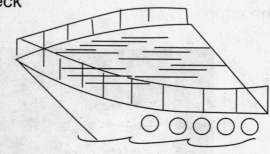

top

column

letter

horn

bat

At Home: Ask students to choose two of the words above. Have them write a paragraph using both meanings of each word.

192

Book 3.2/Unit 3
The Bat Boy and His Violin

Draw Conclusions

A conclusion is what you think about something after you have some information. For the pictures below the conclusions are already supplied. Fill in what you think would be information that would lead to the conclusion.

_____

_____

_____

_____

The boy is a good musician.

_____

_____

_____

_____

Riding a unicycle is difficult.

_____

_____

_____

_____

The tea is hot!

At Home: Invite students to think about conclusions they've made and what information they used to come to the conclusions.

McGraw-Hill School Division

Vocabulary

| bitter | crystal | gripped | kingdom | vanished | whirling |

Write a paragraph about a make-believe kingdom. Use as many vocabulary words from the box as you can. Then erase the vocabulary words or cover them with tape. Give your paragraph to a partner and take your partner's paragraph. Fill in the blanks.

Story Comprehension

Why do you think the ants in "Two Bad Ants" left the group? Would the story have been different if they stayed with the group? Did they learn something by leaving the group and having their adventure? Make up an adventure for the two ants that **wasn't** in the story. Draw a picture to illustrate your adventure story.

At Home: Have students think about what the ants learned by the end of the story and write what they think it was.

194–195

Book 3.2/Unit 3
Two Bad Ants

Do an Author and Title Search

Suppose you wanted to do a report on Laura Ingalls Wilder and her books. How would you do it? Imagine you are at the library in front of the computer. After logging in and typing the author's name, here are some screens that may come up. How would you use them?

Wilder, Laura Ingalls
Laura Ingalls Wilder & Little House Reviews
Laura Ingalls Wilder Series Books
Laura Ingalls Wilder - Books about
Laura Ingalls Wilder Background Articles
Laura Ingalls Wilder Medal

Titles by Laura Ingalls Wilder
Little House in the Big Woods
Little House on the Prairie
Farmer Boy
On the Banks of Plum Creek
By the Shores of Silver Lake
The Long Winter
Little Town on the Prairie
These Happy Golden Years
The First Four Years
On the Way Home
West From Home

About Wilder, Laura Ingalls
Laura's Album: A Remembrance Scrapbook
West From Home: Letters from Laura Ingalls Wilder, San Francisco, 1915
Laura Ingalls Wilder: A Biography
Pioneer Girl: The Story of Laura Ingalls Wilder

Describe how you would use the information on each computer screen for your report on Laura Ingalls Wilder. Use extra paper if necessary.

_____

_____

_____

_____

_____

_____

_____

At Home: Have students pick a subject to explore. Have them write what they did to find the information.

Draw Conclusions

Do the two bad ants act like real ants? Explore the facts before you draw any conclusions.

Fill in the chart showing how the story ants are like and unlike real ants.

All About Ants

Two Bad Ants	Real Ants
live in a colony	_____
obey the queen	_____
eat sugar	_____
_____	_____
_____	_____

Do the two bad ants act like real ants? Write your conclusions here. Use the information on the chart to back up what you say.

_____

_____

_____

Write two questions you still have about ants. Look in the encyclopedia or in a book about ants for the answers.

_____

_____

_____

_____

_____

At Home: Ask students to decide if the story would be better if the ants were more like real ants.

Book 3.2/Unit 3
Two Bad Ants

197

Author's Purpose, Point of View

Everyone sees the world from a different point of view. Animals see the world from a very different point of view. Write a short story about an animal that comes into the classroom. What does it see? What does it think? Draw a picture that illustrates your story.

_____

_____

_____

_____

_____

_____

_____

_____

_____

_____

_____

Book 3.2/Unit 3
Two Bad Ants

At Home: Have students describe their school as if they have just arrived for the first time.

Context Clues

To the ants in "Two Bad Ants," sugar was a sea of crystal, a mouth was a cave, and a faucet was a waterfall. These everyday items seemed strange to the ants because they didn't live in our world.

Below are some everyday items. Imagine the ants saw these things for the first time. List ways these things might be seen by someone who isn't familiar with our world.

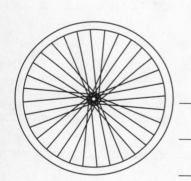
_____
_____
_____
_____

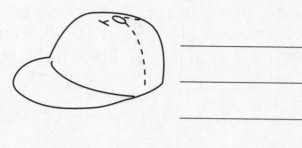
_____
_____
_____
_____
_____

_____
_____
_____
_____

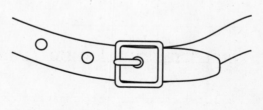
_____
_____
_____
_____

At Home: Have students choose an object from home and think of a new use for the object. Have them write how it would be used.

McGraw-Hill School Division

Make Inferences

Play "Pass the Story." Get together with a group of your classmates. Each member of the group needs a piece of paper and a pen or pencil. One person should keep track of the time. When that person says "Go," each member of the group should begin writing a story. It can be about anything.

After five minutes, the person keeping time should call out "Pass." Then, everyone passes his or her paper to the person to the right. Each person writes again, this time continuing the story that he or she now has taken. After five minutes, "Pass" is called again and the papers get passed to the right again. You can read as much of the story as you like before writing your part.

Continue this way until the story gets back to the person who started it. Then take turns reading the stories aloud.

What happens in the story you began?

_____

_____

_____

Write your beginning sentence again.

Write the rest of the story using your own ideas.

At Home: Have students read the first page of a book from the library. Then have them write what they think will follow. Have them read a few more pages to see if they were close.

Vocabulary

| brain | communicate | crafty | social | solve | subject |

Write a paragraph about a smart animal you know. First, list four or five things you know the animal can do. Use as many of the words in the box as you can. Read your paragraph to another student. Ask the student if he or she has any ideas about improving your paragraph.

Story Comprehension

Some animals communicate without using any sounds. Get together with a partner. Write out what you want to say. It can be anything you feel like. Each of you should stand, facing one another. Then say what you wrote down without speaking. Watch your partner and see if you can understand what he or she is trying to "say." Then each of you can write what you think the other is saying. Share what you wrote and see how close you are.

What I want to say: _____

_____

What I think my partner is saying: _____

_____

At Home: Have students make a list of expressions that human beings make when they are thinking.

201–202

Book 3.2/Unit 3
Do Animals Think?

McGraw-Hill School Division

Use an Encyclopedia Index

An encyclopedia is full of information. A fast way to find that information is with the index. Think of an animal you would like to learn about. Go to the back of the encyclopedia. Find the name of the animal you've chosen. Which pages are listed? Go to those pages and read about the animal.

Use what you have learned to draw a detailed picture of the animal below. Summarize the information to write a caption to go with the picture.

Caption: _____

_____

_____

McGraw-Hill School Division

Book 3.2/Unit 3
Do Animals Think?

At Home: Ask students to think of a topic they would like to learn about. Have them explain how they would use an encyclopedia index to get information on this topic.

203

Make Inferences

If you know certain facts about animals you can make inferences. For instance, you know that dolphins live in the sea, so you can infer that dolphins know how to swim.

Below are some facts about animals. Write what you can infer from the facts listed.

1. Ants live together in colonies.

_____

_____

_____

2. Lions hunt other animals.

_____

_____

_____

3. Duck feathers repel water.

_____

_____

_____

At Home: Have students list some of the foods they eat. Ask them: What inferences could someone make about you based on what you eat? Have them write out their thoughts.

204

Book 3.2/Unit 3
Do Animals Think?

Form Generalizations

Generalizations are based on examples. What are some generalizations you can make about Samuel based on the pictures above?

_____

_____

_____

_____

_____

_____

Book 3.2/Unit 3
Do Animals Think?

At Home: Have students think of some generalizations that are
true for them. Have them write down a few of these
generalizations.

205

Multiple-Meaning Words

Some words have the same spelling and pronunciation but different meanings. Read the words below. Write down two phrases that use each word two different ways.

bat _____

_____

deck _____

_____

lap _____

_____

cap _____

_____

Then draw a funny picture. Choose a word. Take part of the first meaning and combine it with part of the second meaning. See what you come up with.

At Home: Help students make a list of multiple-meaning words.

206

Book 3.2/Unit 3
Do Animals Think?

McGraw-Hill School Division

Draw Conclusions

Use the information given to draw conclusions. Write your conclusions in the space provided.

1. Aunt Dot is keeping a secret from Lonnie.
Lonnie's birthday is in two days.
Aunt Dot is calling Lonnie's friends.

Conclusion: _____

_____

2. Bert feeds his dog, Dutchie, every day.
Bert's dog hasn't eaten all day.
It's almost time to go to bed.

Conclusion: _____

_____

3. Eric is going to play a part in a play.
Tomorrow the class is putting on a play.
Eric tells his mother he's very busy.

Conclusion: _____

_____

Exchange your conclusions with a partner. Do you like his or her conclusions better? Why or why not?

_____

_____

_____

McGraw-Hill School Division

Book 3.2/Unit 3
"Wilbur's Boast" from
Charlotte's Web

At Home: Have students look at pictures in newspapers and draw conclusions about what is happening based on the information in the pictures. Then have them read the article to see if they were right.

207

Vocabulary

| considering | conversation | boasting | hesitated | interrupted | seized |

Use some of the words above to make up or retell the beginning and middle of a fairy tale. Do not write the end. Exchange papers with a partner. Finish the tale. Does your partner like your ending? Do you like your partner's ending?

Story Comprehension

Work with a group to put on a play. The characters can be Charlotte, Wilbur, Templeton, and the lamb. Decide who will play each character. Make up a scene like the one you read, but change what Wilbur tries to do. Add words of your own. Rehearse the scene with your group. Then act it out for the rest of the class.

At Home: Have students think of something they are especially good at and write about their ability, explaining how they do what they do.

Book 3.2/Unit 3
"Wilbur's Boast" from
Charlotte's Web

McGraw-Hill School Division

Do an Electronic Subject Search

Computers can help you find information quickly. It helps if you can narrow down the subject you want to explore. Look at each computer screen. Circle words you would use to find out about the subject named on top.

raising piglets
?
farms
raising
Wilbur
Pigs

black widow spiders
?
animals
widows
spiders
black

E. B. White
?
colors
authors
White
Charlotte

Pick a subject you want to know about. Then do your own search in the library. Write a short paragraph about how you did the research.

_____

_____

_____

_____

_____

_____

_____

_____

_____

_____

Book 3.2/Unit 3
"Wilbur's Boast" from
Charlotte's Web

At Home: Have students make a list of likely subject headings for topics they want to explore.

210

Draw Conclusions

Do the animals in "Wilbur's Boast" act like real animals? Explore the facts before you draw conclusions. Take a look in an encyclopedia or do a subject search in the library.

Make a chart showing how the animals in the story are like and unlike real animals.

	Like	**Unlike**
Charlotte	_____	_____
	_____	_____
	_____	_____
Wilbur	_____	_____
	_____	_____
	_____	_____
Templeton	_____	_____
	_____	_____
	_____	_____

Add drawings to illustrate your work.

Do the animals act like real animals? Write your conclusions here.

_____

_____

_____

At Home: Have students discuss how the conclusions they made changed after they did the research.

211

Book 3.2/Unit 3
"Wilbur's Boast" from
Charlotte's Web

McGraw-Hill School Division

Form Generalizations

Match the generalization below with the examples and facts that back up the statement. Write the letter or letters on the line.

1. Mr. Brown likes pancakes.

   _____

2. Monkeys are smart animals.

   _____

3. Jerry plays the piano.

   _____

4. Natasha has pet goldfish.

   _____

5. Boris is going on a hike.

   _____

6. Dee Dee knows how to dance.

   _____

a. Natasha wears a blue hat.

b. Dee Dee teaches dance lessons at the community center.

c. Mr. Brown goes to work every day.

d. Boris is studying trail maps.

e. Monkeys can be taught languages.

f. Natasha buys goldfish food once a week.

g. Jerry plays piano at school concerts.

h. Boris is packing his backpack.

i. The neighbors hear Jerry practice the piano.

j. Mr. Brown eats pancakes every day.

McGraw-Hill School Division

Book 3.2/Unit 3
"Wilbur's Boast" from
Charlotte's Web

At Home: Have students make generalizations about characters in stories they enjoy.

212

Context Clues

Sometimes a word's **context,** the way it is used in a sentence, can help to make its meaning clear. What do you think the made-up word in each cartoon below means? Write your answers on the lines.

1. clacky _____

2. snorking _____

3. poder _____

4. griffy _____

Now it's your turn to make up words. Write a new word for each meaning below.

1. walking backwards _____

2. a ruined dinner _____

At Home: Play a version of Twenty Questions with students. Take turns making up words and answering yes/no questions to discover what each word means.

213

Book 3.2/Unit 3
"Wilbur's Boast" from
Charlotte's Web

McGraw-Hill School Division

Author's Purpose, Point of View

What's your favorite subject? What are some facts you know about the subject? Pick a subject and make a list of at least five facts. If you don't know that many, do some research in an encyclopedia or at the library. List the subject and the facts below.

Subject: _____

Facts: _____

_____

_____

_____

_____

A good writer makes facts interesting. Prepare a presentation for the class. Think of a fun or entertaining way to inform the class. You can use props such as pictures or masks. You can even make up jokes! Write out what you want to say and then give your presentation to the class.

McGraw-Hill School Division

At Home: Have students cut out articles in magazines or newspapers that inform in interesting ways.

Vocabulary

crates	loops	rescuers	snug	starve	strip

Make up a story using the above words. Be the hero of the story. Make it as exciting as you can. Write it out and present it to the class.

Story Comprehension

Reread "The Koala Catchers" so that you know all about koalas. Then find the koalas in the picture. Write a koala fact next to each one.

At Home: Have students find pictures of animals from magazines and newspapers, then cut them out to make an animal zoo poster.

McGraw-Hill School Division

Use a Resource

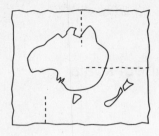  

You are a magazine editor preparing a photo essay on Australia. You have the photos, but you need some facts for the captions. Write questions about Australia that you might find answered in each resource below.

Dictionary: _____

_____

Encyclopedia: _____

_____

Internet: _____

_____

Newspaper: _____

_____

Telephone directory: _____

_____

Look in a resource for an answer to your question. Write what you find.

_____

_____

At Home: Have students cut out magazine pictures related to a subject of their choice. They can arrange and paste these on paper, then look up information in various research resources to use in writing captions.

Form Generalizations

Think about the people in "The Koala Catchers." What kind of generalizations can you make about them?

Start with the facts. Make a list of everything you know about koala catchers. Include quotes, too.

_____

_____

_____

_____

_____

_____

_____

_____

_____

_____

_____

_____

_____

From the information you have listed, write a description on another piece of paper of what you think the koala catchers are like. Use the facts to back up what you say. Then write a generalization about koala catchers below.

_____

_____

At Home: Have students make generalizations about koalas.
Ask them to give facts to back up their generalization.

218

Book 3.2/Unit 3
The Koala Catchers

McGraw-Hill School Division

Context Clues

Look at the pictures below. Then write what the characters may be saying.

Draw your own pictures that show what people may be thinking or feeling.
Exchange with a partner to figure out the clues.

At Home: Have students look through magazines for
photographs of people, cut them out, and write captions
that tell what the people may be saying.

Multiple-Meaning Words

On the left are some examples of multiple-meaning words used in a sentence. Fill in the blanks on the right side with the words in dark type from the left side.

The meat was very **lean.**

I always **part** my hair.

She put on her best **dress.**

The **top** spun around and around.

He could **smell** the bacon.

Everyone tries to ———— like her.

The ———— of the mountain was invisible.

Don't ———— against the railing.

The actor was believable in the

————.

The ———— made me feel sick.

Pick a word in dark type. Draw a picture to illustrate both its meanings. You may use captions if you wish. Then write some more multiple-meaning words that you know.

At Home: Have students find multiple-meaning words in newspaper articles and use them to create a multiple-meaning scrapbook.

220

Book 3.2/Unit 3
The Koala Catchers

McGraw-Hill School Division

Vocabulary Review

Use markers to play this game with a partner. Flip a coin. **Heads,** move 1 space. **Tails,** move 2 spaces. Use the word you land on in a sentence. Take turns. The one who reaches **End** first is the winner.

start   end

equipment	considering	conversation	strip
perform	subject	boasting	starve
talented	solve	hesitated	snug
crystal	brain	interrupted	rescuers
gripped	whirling	crates	loops

At Home: Have students write the words in the box on cards, then pick a card and use the word to make up a riddle.

Name_____ Date_____ **Extend** ◆222◆

Vocabulary Review

Plan a story with a partner. Use animals as your main characters. First, list six things that will happen in the story. Then use the words in the box to describe the characters or to tell what they do.

kingdom	vanished	accept	bitter	invisible
mistakes	communicate	crafty	social	seized

_____

_____

_____

_____

_____

_____

_____

_____

_____

_____

_____

_____

_____

_____

At Home: Have students write a nonfiction story with real characters, including family, friends, pets, or others, using as many of the words in the box as they can.

Book 3.2/Unit 3

222